TELLING TALES:
A STUDENT GUIDE TO THE AQA GCSE SHORT STORY ANTHOLOGY

NATALIE TWIGG

&

DAVID WHEELER

Red Axe Books

ISBN: 978-0993218361

Find us at:

www.dogstailbooks.co.uk

CONTENTS

'Chemistry' - Graham Swift

Author

Novelist Graham Swift is a Fellow of the Royal Society of Literature. He was born in London in 1949, educated at Dulwich College, Cambridge and York Universities and is the author of several novels. *Waterland*, published in 1983, won the *Guardian* Fiction Prize and the Geoffrey Faber Memorial Prize. It concerns his youth spent in the Norfolk Fens during the Second World War and is narrated by history teacher, Tom Crick. Since publication it has established itself as one of the classics of twentieth-century British Literature. The short story, *Chemistry*, was taken from Swift's collection of short stories 'Learning to Swim'. The collection explores the complexities of familial life: 'An admirable collection. Each story has its subtle nuances of narrative and language which establishes a quite distinct character. A most impressive work of Fiction' *The Times.*

In an article for The Guardian, published in July this year, Swift said of the short story, in relation to novels:

Practitioners of the short story are apt to say it's the more challenging form, partly so they can claim it requires superior skill, and partly, in defence, to explain why readers aren't as keen on them as on novels – though that may be just feeding a myth. More challenging to write? Possibly, but in turning recently, after such a long gap, from novels to short stories I didn't feel I'd become a different, more challenged creature. If anything, the opposite. I felt refreshed, happily reconnected with the writer of short stories I once was.

Context

'Chemistry', written in first person narrative, is a reflection on family tragedy which occurred in the narrator's formative years. Following the death of the central character's father and grandmother, mother (the grandfather's daughter), child and grandfather live together as a family unit. At first, the 'equation' of family life seems to work, until Ralph, mother's new boyfriend, upsets family dynamics. The grandfather, who becomes ostracised by the mother's refocused attentions (toward Ralph) and by Ralph's own hostility towards him, retreats to his garden shed where he conducts chemical experiments. The protagonist child, who is ten years old, joins his grandfather in his isolation where he learns the rudimentary aspects of chemistry. The story concludes with the third and final tragedy of this family's life, the apparent suicide of the grandfather.

'Chemistry' explores the relationship between the living and the dead, appearance and reality, loyalty and betrayal as well as familial rivalry and grief. It also explores the delicacy of family dynamics and how, as with chemistry itself, subtle imbalances can have cataclysmic results.

Plot

The story is divided into eleven Sections (dependent upon the copy you are reading, this may be denoted by a series of dots or double lined spaces). In the first Section the protagonist fondly recalls the times spent with his grandfather and mother at the local pond sailing the boat he and his grandfather had built. The boy explains the appeal of their winter visits within the parenthesis: "We would go even in the winter – especially in the winter, because then we would have the pond to ourselves – when the leaves on the two willows turned yellow…." This instantly suggests an exclusivity in the trio's relationship and within the same paragraph the protagonist uses the boat's trajectory as a metaphor for their bond:

As it moved it seemed that it followed an actual existing line between Grandfather, myself and Mother, as if Grandfather were pulling it toward him on some invisible cord, and he had to do this to prove we were not beyond his reach.

The boy then states that 'the voyages were trouble free', before giving an account of the boat sinking, which the protagonist observes coincided with the arrival of Ralph within their family dynamic: "Then one day – it must have been soon after Mother met Ralph – we watched the boat...." The use of parenthesis here suggests that Ralph's arrival and the boat sinking were not incidental; it provides a metaphor for Ralph's detrimental influence on familial relations, certainly from the narrator's perspective and it is almost as if Ralph is responsible for the boat sinking.

Despite the Grandfather's attempts at retrieving the boat, we learn that it is not salvageable which provides a foreshadowing to the family's eventual demise. The boy describes it as 'the first loss of my life that I had witnessed', the grandfather tells the boy that "You must accept it – you can't get it back – it's the only way." He observes at this stage that his Mother's face is 'very still and very white' as if she 'had seen something appalling'. Again, this is a foreshadowing of revelations to come.

In Section 2 we learn that Ralph is now a regular fixture at home and tensions are escalating. When the grandfather addresses his daughter observing that: "You don't make curry any more, the way you did for Alec, the way Vera taught you." (Referring to his deceased wife and son-in-law), Ralph responds with: "Why don't you leave her alone?!" Ralph then seems to attempt usurping the grandfather in his familial role by offering to buy the boy a new boat, the boy responds with a strident "no". It is clear from this Section that family 'chemistry' has already become altered by the arrival of this new character. It is also clear that the narrator, the boy, is reluctant to accept Ralph or the altered family dynamics.

In Section 3 Swift describes the circumstances leading to the trio's arrangements prior to Ralph. Grandfather had been working for a company who manufactured gold and silver-plated items; his wife died suddenly when his grandson was four. Following her death, which he took badly, the grandfather 'needed the company of his daughter'; this in turn created marital tension between the mother and father. The grandfather refused to leave his house which he ceased to maintain and spent increasing amounts of time in his shed. We learn that there was 'bitterness all around' which was resolved in a 'dreadful way': '...by my own father's death'. The protagonist's father had died in a light aircraft crash in 'unexceptional' weather conditions whilst crossing the Irish Sea, just three years after his grandmother's death. The boy goes on to explain that this united his mother and grandfather in a 'sad symmetry' of mutual grief – the widow and the widower both of whom had lost their respective spouses suddenly and unexpectedly. Following her husband's death the mother sold the house and the three moved in together.

Section 3 also refers to the physical familial similarities amongst the family, specifically between the living and the dead and the emotional power these resemblances have. At the start of the Section the boy observes his grandfather gazing 'curiously into my face'.

We learn that this family, reconstructed in grief, were happy but isolated from the outside world: "we scarcely made contact with the outside world." We also learn that the grandfather had begun to treat his daughter like a wife: she was prevented from working and was the recipient of bracelets and earrings: "He kept mother and me like he might have kept his own wife and son."

Swift then returns to the incident with the boat, a tacit reference to the arrival of Ralph, when happiness appears to have been lost: "...that day in the park when my boat, setting out across the pond towards Grandfather, sank." The trajectory of the boat and the invisible lines linking the family were used in Section 1 as a metaphor for the familial ties which bound this irregular family. The boat sinking therefore expands on this metaphor; its demise can also be seen as the end of an era for mother, grandfather and boy.

In Section 4 Swift describes the strained new dynamics following Ralph's arrival. We learn that he is a big man 'who ate heartily'; the boy is intimidated by him and fears that he might be hit. Equally, he is scared that his grandfather's provocation of Ralph will end in violence. The mother appears to placate the situation and 'somehow kept him [Ralph] in check'. However, it appears that in order to do so the mother has become neglectful of her father: she no longer cooks his favourite dishes; she is hurtful. The boy identifies this as his mother's way of demonstrating her allegiance to Ralph. Despite these tensions, the boy - now reflecting as an adult, concludes that all three: mother, grandfather and child, still clung to 'this delicate equilibrium that she, he and I had constructed over the months'.

In Section 5 tensions escalate further as the grandfather deliberately eats slowly in order to provoke Ralph; this culminates in Ralph's outburst: "For Christ's sake we're not waiting all night for him to finish!." The mother ushers her son into the kitchen and gripping his shoulders asks rhetorically: "What are we going to do?" Her complicity with her child, in the face of Ralph's behaviour, leads the protagonist to the false assumption that they will unite against Ralph: "I had a feeling of being back in that old impregnable domain which Ralph had not yet penetrated." The protagonist also shares with the reader that "inside I was starting to form a plan." However, on returning to the dinner table the mother clearly sides with Ralph.

In Section 6 Swift invites the reader into the grandfather's shed: 'Grandfather's shed was more than just a shed'. We learn that the shed is more like a miniature home, with a stove, an armchair and all the apparatus required to conduct his chemical experiments. Before Ralph's arrival we discover that the protagonist had always thought of his grandfather's shed as a private place. However, on this occasion the boy feels that the green door of the shed is extending him a silent invitation, one which only he could read. His grandfather greets him with: "I thought you would come."

In Section 7 the protagonist describes how his mother's action of 'driving' his grandfather out culminated in him being taught the fundamentals of chemistry: 'I would watch Grandfather's experiments. I would ask him to explain what he was doing and to name the contents of his various bottles'. The shed provides sanctuary from the menacing place home has become ('I felt safe in his shed'); the boy then describes how Ralph's behaviour has evolved in the relative absence of his grandfather – he has taken to eating ever bigger meals and 'lording' it up. Meanwhile, within the asylum of the shed, the boy sees his grandfather for who he truly is, not the 'sour' and 'cantankerous' man he was in the house but '…a weary, ailing man…'.

In Section 8 the conversation between grandfather and grandchild revolves around the nature of chemistry; the grandfather explains that chemistry is not about creation but about alteration: "…chemistry is the science of change. You don't make things in chemistry – you change them. Anything you can change." The grandfather expands upon this theme with: "Hydrochloric acid and nitric acid. Neither would work by itself, but the mixture will." Swift leads the reader to wonder whether the caustic elements the grandfather refers to are metaphors for his daughter and Ralph, whose interaction and mutual complicity have culminated in both the grandfather's exile and the grandson's unease. It is the child who takes this metaphor to the next level asking his grandfather "people change too, don't they?" When the grandfather confirms that people do change but the elements remain the same the boy is struck by a strange sensation. He envisages his grandfather's face as being cut from an 'infinite stick of rock', from which his mother's and his own face may also be cut: 'I had a giddying feeling that there is no end to anything'. The Section concludes with the child, uneasy with the concept of infinity, returning to simple questions requiring 'simple' 'precise' facts. Pointing to a jar of clear liquid, the boy questions the contents, the grandfather replies with "Laurel water. Prussic Acid'. He smiled. 'Not for drinking…"

Section 9 introduces the basis for the boy's plan referred to obliquely in Section 5. Swift chooses to open the paragraph with 'it was an exceptionally cold Autumn, a metaphor, perhaps, for the escalating frostiness within the family. We learn that the boy has been tasked with removing grandfather's dinner plate from the shed after he has eaten. On returning to the house, the child now often sees his mother and Ralph in a drunken torpor. At first the mother had resisted alcohol, conveying her disapproval, but now she appears to have joined Ralph: 'The drink made Mother go soft and heavy and blurred and it made Ralph gain authority'. The boy observes that Ralph's physical presence, 'his big lurching frame... enveloping her...' makes his mother appear 'trapped and helpless'. From the boy's perspective we are led to believe that this coupling is not a relationship of equals: Ralph has all the power. This provides the first justification for the protagonist's ensuing actions. The second justification comes in the form of the grandfather's altered demeanour: 'In his slumber – his hair dishevelled, mouth open – he looked like some torpid, captive animal that had lost even the will to eat...' The protagonist sees both his mother and grandfather as 'helpless' victims of Ralph, they are 'trapped' and 'captive' in this altered life, he is therefore compelled to act in their defence. Section 10 expands upon this further.

Having removed some HNO (acid) from his grandfather's shed at the end of Section 9, the boy's machination is revealed – he intends to throw the acid into Ralph's face the following morning. We learn that he has no intention of killing Ralph: he merely wishes to disfigure him. The boy reveals that he has difficulty sleeping until he is sure that his grandfather has returned to the house; this particular night though he does not remember his grandfather returning.

During the night the narrator reveals that his father appeared before him as an apparition. He tells his son: "It was her. She made a hole in the bottom of the boat, not big enough to notice, so it would sink – so you and Grandfather would watch it sink. The boat sank – like my plane." His father therefore implies that the boy's mother was responsible not just for the boat's sinking but for his own untimely death; ultimately, for the demise of the whole family. It is not clear whether this is a dream or an actual visitation from the afterlife but the boy clearly believes the latter – when the father questions whether the boy believes him, the boy replies with: "Yes. I believe you. I'll prove it." Remember in Section 1 the boy glimpsed something in his mother's face: 'It was very still and very white, as if she had seen something appalling." At the outset he had a suspicion as to his mother's involvement in the sinking of the boat. This apprehension serves to strengthen the notion.

The next morning the third and final tragedy plays out – the death of the grandfather. The boy watches as his grandfather's body is carried to an ambulance with Ralph overseeing manoeuvres like someone directing 'the loading of some vital piece of cargo'. This dehumanisation of his grandfather's body serves to highlight Ralph's lack of compassion, certainly from the boy's perspective. The Section closes with his mother impassionedly appealing to her son: "Darling. Please. I'll explain. Darling. Darling." The fact that the mother feels the need to explain the grandfather's death suggests, as per the apparition of the father and the foreshadowing in his mother's face in Section 1, some culpability on the mother's part.

Section 11 describes the aftermath of the tragedy. Despite the mother promising to provide the boy with an explanation she remains silent on the matter. The official verdict is that the grandfather committed suicide by swallowing prussic acid: 'But all other things that should have been explained – or confessed – she never did explain." The boy sees in his mother's face 'relief' rather than grief: 'as if she had recovered from an illness'. The narrator also describes his mother's actions shortly after the funeral: 'she went into Grandfather's bedroom and flung wide the windows. It was a brilliant, crisp-November day... And she said: "There isn't that lovely?" Similarly, as they are standing at the graveside the boy observes his mother's lack of tears. Each of these elements suggests a boy assessing his mother's blameworthiness: she provides no explanation as to grandfather's death, she describes the day as 'lovely' despite the tragedy which has taken place shortly before and she remains dry-eyed at the funeral. The implication is that his mother is both dishonest and dispassionate, someone who has quite literally succeeded in getting away with murder.

At the coroner's court the ten year-old protagonist is not expected to contribute but he is desperate to speak out and we learn that his concept of murder is sufficiently flexible to include two scenarios: direct administration of the poison by his mother and/or creating a home life in which tensions and hostilities may have forced his grandfather to take his own life: 'I wanted to tell them – about how Mother had banished Grandfather, about how suicide can be murder...' Fearing that he will be implicated himself, he disposes of the jar of HNO.

In this Section the narrator describes the new family in derisive terms, he considers the altered kin-ship to be phoney, a poor version of his former family: 'We stood at the ceremony, Mother, Ralph and I, like a mock version of the trio – Grandfather, Mother and I...'

After the funeral Ralph and the boy's mother appear to rise from their torpor and are driven to action in the form of disposing of grandfather's personal effects, clearing the overgrown garden and clipping back the trees. We learn that the house will be sold and Ralph will buy them a new one. This leaves the boy feeling he has 'nowhere to go' and so he returns to the pond, the place at which he had felt most content after his father's death. The author then introduces the second apparition, that of the boy's grandfather: 'He was smiling, and I knew the launch was still travelling over to him... along that invisible line. And his hands, his acid-marked hands, would reach out and receive it'. This concluding line returns to the concept of infinity touched upon in Section 8, something which, at the time, the boy was troubled by: 'I had a giddying feeling that there is no end to anything'. In light of his family's radically altered state it appears, at the end of this story, that the boy now takes comfort from this. The metaphors of the 'invisible stick of rock' and the 'invisible line' continue to bind the family even after death.

Characters

The boy

As we know, the story is written exclusively in the first person narrative: this means that all the details we are party to come from one single perspective, that of the boy who is now an adult; the story consists of his reflections on a series of family tragedies.

In Section 3 he refers to 'my childish assumptions.., from this it is clear he is no longer a child. His age is indeterminate but the sophisticated language he uses and his choice of words are certainly not that of a 10 year old boy; the text is rich with alliteration, in Section 3 the boy recalls life before Ralph: 'For about a year we lived quietly, calmly even contentedly within the scope of this sad symmetry'. Later in the same Section he recollects: '...and for a whole year, a whole harmonious year, we were really quite happy'. In addition, the character reveals through the text a mature affinity with nature, often observing the changing seasons and the impact this has on his surroundings. In Section 10 he observes: '...heavy rain and the tossing branches of the rowan tree....' In Section 11: 'It was a brilliant, crisp, late-November day and the leaves on the rowan tree were all gold...' Earlier in the text, in Section 5, the boy refers to the changing seasons: 'Through the window, half visible in the twilight, the evergreen shrubs which filled our garden were defying the onset of Autumn...' These are not the observations of a child, they are the reflective recollections of an adult.

As an adult, we know very little about this character, the story concerns his childhood and we know that because he chooses to recount this particular story its events must have been extremely seminal to his adult life. Swift has written this story almost as if it is a confessional on the boy's part; he (the boy, now an adult) appears to be imploring the reader to provide answers; answers which his mother was unable to supply. The boy, though naive, is acutely aware of the dynamics and strains between the adults in his life. In Section 1 the boy describes the relationship between himself, his mother and grandfather, using the boat as a metaphor: 'As it moved it seemed that it followed an actual existing line between Grandfather, myself and Mother, as if Grandfather were pulling us toward him on some invisible cord, and that he had to do this to prove we were not beyond his reach...' This demonstrates a profound awareness of their familial bond.

In Section 3 the narrator recalls how family dynamics were changed by the death of his grandmother; the boy is aware of tensions but does not quite understand them: 'There was bitterness all around, which I scarcely appreciated'. When Ralph comes onto the scene, the boy observes his mother's neglect of his grandfather: '...she would cook the things that Ralph liked... and forget to produce the meals that Grandfather was fond of....' This, the boy sees, as his mother demonstrating her 'allegiance to Ralph...' Throughout the story we are spectators to an adult trying both to understand the grown-ups of his younger life and the events which occurred during that time.

The boy is exclusively surrounded by adults; there is no mention of any other children. In this sense he perhaps has a heightened awareness of tensions amongst his family. Even in play, with the boat, his interactions are limited to the exclusivity of his grandfather. When tensions escalate between grandfather and Ralph his mother turns to him for an adult solution asking him the possibly rhetorical question: "What am I going to do?", the text further reveals that his mother had asked him the same question when his father had died.

When the boy describes Ralph we learn that he is a large man who 'lords' it up (Section 7) in the house. He has encouraged his mother to drink with him; the boy sees this as a means of controlling his mother: 'The drink made mother go soft and heavy and blurred and it made Ralph gain in authority'. In Section 7 the boy divulges: 'I felt safe in his shed. The house where Ralph now lorded it....was a menacing place'.

The child the adult narrator describes is reflective and empathetic, however, his quiet resistance to Ralph and his doubts over his mother's involvement in both his father and grandfather's deaths reveals a less than trusting nature. The boy is estranged from other children and the distraction that provides and is therefore confronted with purely adult issues and interactions. The adult voice does not refer to any adult relationships he may have formed over the intervening years which suggests that he remains isolated, perhaps unable to move on in life without an adequate explanation of the events which occurred in his childhood.

The mother

The boy, or young adult, could be perceived as an unreliable narrator - the events he describes are emotionally charged and he is the only voice in this story; additionally the events which occurred happened some years before - as such, the people in the story are presented from a one-dimensional perspective, based upon childhood recollections.

The mother, the narrator describes, is largely a passive character; even in the first Section she does not involve herself in play with the child - she would 'sit on a wooden bench set back from the perimeter'. In

Section 3 the boy discloses the fact that his grandfather would not let his mother work, even after he had reached retirement age, again this suggests passivity on the mother's part and is a fairly reliable fact rather than a point of view. When Ralph enters into the family's life the mother 'grows neglectful' (Section 4) of grandfather, although the child observes 'she wouldn't have forgiven someone else's hurting him'. However, we learn in this Section that the mother no longer cooks his grandfather's favourite foods, preferring to please Ralph with his culinary preferences instead. In Section 5 tensions peak. Grandfather is eating deliberately slowly to incite Ralph, Ralph then turns to his mother saying: "For Christ''s sake, we're not waiting all night for him to finish!." Ralph's rude outburst presents an opportunity for the mother to intervene, to demonstrate her allegiance to the grandfather. However, instead of defending her father: '...Mother drove him out...' (Section 7). These events are suggestive of a weak woman and later, despite being disapproving of alcohol (Section 9), she starts to partake in Ralph's drinking: 'The drink made Mother go soft and heavy and blurred and it made Ralph gain in authority'. The boy describes how his mother looks 'trapped' and 'helpless', yet she makes no protest and seems resigned to this role of subservience.

The narrator suggests that as well as being subservient and passive there may also be an element of malevolence to the mother. The apparition of his father, which appears in Section 10, implicates his mother in the sinking of the ship: 'It was her. She made a hole in the bottom of the boat, not big enough for anyone to notice, so it would sink - so you and Grandfather would watch it sink....' In the concluding paragraph the boy himself implicates his mother in his grandfather's death, suggesting that the quality of family life had been instrumental in the suicide: '...Though there was a thousand things I wanted to tell them - about how Mother banished Grandfather, about how suicide can be murder...' (Section 11).

We know that the mother refers to her son as her 'little man' (Section

3) and that she turns to him in difficult times. In Section 5, after the meal incident when Ralph becomes irate with grandfather, she addresses her son: "What am I going to do?" - we learn that she asked the same question of him after the death of her husband with 'the same quivery look of being about to spill over'. (Section 5) There is no demonstration at any point of maternal protection, she makes no attempt to shelter her son from adult stresses and, despite promising to provide an explanation as to grandfather's death, we know that even when the boy reaches maturity the explanation remains unvoiced: 'All her life then, I think, she has been trying to explain, or to avoid explaining... all the other things which should have been explained - or confessed - she never did'. (Section 11). Through the mother's parenting omissions, the boy is exposed to adult matters. This in turn could be seen as denying him the right to a healthy childhood. The very fact that the story concerns an adult still trying to make sense of his childhood reveals the damage his mother has caused.

Finally, when the 'suicide' verdict is disclosed, as mentioned in the Plot Section, the boy sees in his mother's face 'relief' rather than grief: 'as if she had recovered from an illness'. The narrator also describes his mother's actions shortly after the funeral: 'she went into Grandfather's bedroom and flung wide the windows. It was a brilliant, crisp-November day... And she said: "There isn't that lovely?." Similarly, as they are standing at the graveside the boy observes his mother's lack of tears. The implication is that his mother is both insensitive to her child's grief and emotionally removed from her own father's death, perhaps even culpable.

The grandfather

The grandfather, a complex character, represents the lynchpin to the family, prior to Ralph's arrival. The first Section describes a man heavily involved with his grandson; we learn that he and his grandson regularly play with the little plywood boat which they made together. Later in Section 7 the grandfather teaches his grandson 'the fundamentals of chemistry'. From this we can assume that the grandfather is a tolerant and empathetic man - not all adults have the patience to spend time with young children. However, as the story progresses more negative traits are revealed; we learn that he is quite an obstinate man and perhaps a little controlling himself. When his wife dies he demands time of his daughter but refuses to leave his house. This creates tensions between the boy's parents, which we now know were 'resolved' by the father's death. Similarly, after Ralph's arrival, the grandfather makes a concerted effort to eat slowly, antagonising Ralph: 'He deliberately ate slowly to provoke Ralph'. (Section 5). From the boy's recollection, in Section 3, it transpires that the grandfather's obstinacy and need for control meant that after the deaths of grandmother and father, his mother was not permitted to work. Additionally, the bereaved family (after the deaths of grandmother and father) - mother, grandfather and boy (who were 'reconciled in mutual grief' Section 3) represent an odd grouping, one in which traditional familial roles are blurred: 'We forgot we were three generations. Grandfather bought Mother bracelets and earrings. Mother called me her 'little man'. We lived for each other...' (Section 3). This is slightly concerning as it suggests that the grandfather is treating his daughter as a proxy wife: the gift of jewellery is generally associated with romance. Swift's use of this device indicates a slightly less savoury element to the grandfather's character. Swift provides further clues as to the grandfather's character flaws in Section 3; after the boy's father's death, and thus the end to those familial tensions, he has the boy recall: 'I don't know if Grandfather took a secret, vengeful delight in my father's death, or if he was capable of it...' This implants the seeds of doubt in the readers' mind.

While the narrative explores the exile of the grandfather from his own home, the reader remains sympathetic – despite the aforementioned flaws, but later, by the boy's own admission, we learn that the grandfather must take some responsibility for family hostilities himself (Section 7): 'And Grandfather wasn't the same person in his shed as he was in the house – sour and cantankerous'. So despite initially appealing to the reader as a patient and empathetic man, the narrative incrementally reveals an obstinate, controlling, 'sour' and provocative man.

At the end of the short story it is unclear whether or not the grandfather took his own life (we have touched before on the mother's possible culpability). The human response to suicide can manifest as polar opposites; some people believe that it is a singularly selfish act, leaving devastation literally in its wake, while others will regard it as a tragedy. Swift steers us in neither direction and leaves us to draw our own conclusion. In the final Section (11) the narrative describes the boy's mother's response to her father's death; she remains dry-eyed and apparently unmoved. Again, this could suggest one of a number of things: the mother's culpability, her relief at being free from her father's control, or something altogether more sinister about the grandfather (as indicated by the 'romantic' gifts of jewellery). Whether or not the father was physically abusive again remains inconclusive.

Ralph

From the boy's perspective and from his adult recollection Ralph is presented as an idle man, 'lording' it up in the grandfather's house. He is framed as a gluttonous, drinking man with an intolerance of the grandfather: "For Christ's sake we're not waiting all night for him to finish!." (Section 5). He presents a source of fear to the boy ('He was a big man who ate heartily, and I was often afraid he might hit me...' Section 4) and the boy describes the effect he has upon his mother and grandfather: 'She looked trapped and helpless' (Section 9), '...he looked like some torpid, captive animal that has lost even the will to eat...' (Section 9). It is clear that the boy views Ralph's arrival as the end to 'a whole harmonious year, (in which) we were really quite happy...' (Section 3). Through omission we can surmise that Ralph does not work, there is no mention of a trade or career and so we can assume that the grandfather is also funding, not only his daughter and grandson's life, but also Ralph's.

At the beginning of the story Ralph appears to be trying to win the boy's affection, however, he does so in a pecuniary manner by offering to buy him a replacement boat: '...Ralph said to me, as if pouncing on something: 'How about me buying you a new one? How would you like that?." (Section 2). Swift introduces Ralph as a means of destabilising this somewhat unusual family, his presence serves to split the family into two camps of allegiance:

I suppose the question was how far Ralph could tolerate not letting go with Grandfather so as to keep Mother, or how far Mother was prepared to turn against Grandfather so as not to lose Ralph. I remember keeping a sort of equation in my head: if Ralph hurts Grandfather it means I'm right – he doesn't really care about Mother at all; but if Mother is cruel to Grandfather (though she would only be cruel to him because she couldn't forsake him) it means she really loves Ralph. (Section 4).

The father

All we really know of the father is that in life he worked for an importer of Irish goods. He died when the aircraft flying to Cork or Dublin vanished without trace in the Irish Sea, at this time the boy was seven years old. Prior to this the Grandmother had died (when the boy was four) and the grief of both those losses served to unite Mother and Grandfather: '...fate had made him and his daughter quits and reconciled them in mutual grief'. (Section 3), 'For about a year we lived quietly, calmly, even contentedly within the scope of this sad symmetry...' (Section 3).

The father's death presents a source of confusion in the narrator's young mind, he has difficulty accepting his father is gone: 'I wanted to know when he would return. Perhaps I knew, even as I asked this, that he never would, that my childish assumptions were only a way of allaying my own grief. But if I really believed Father was gone for ever – I was wrong'. (Section 3).

The father then appears to the boy as an apparition: 'That night Father came to my bedroom. I knew it was him. His hair and clothes were wet, his lips were caked with salt; seaweed hung from his shoulders...' (Section 10). The apparition of the father then implicates the boy's mother in the sinking of the boat: 'It was her. She made a hole in the bottom of the boat, not big enough to notice, so it would sink – so you and Grandfather would watch it sink. The boat sank – like my plane'. (Section 10). After this accusation and in tandem with the mother's actions following her father's death, the lack of an outward appearance of grief, the boy becomes suspicious of his mother: 'There was a thousand things I wanted to tell them – about how Mother had banished Grandfather, about how suicide can be murder...' (Section 11).

Swift uses the apparition of the father as a means of strengthening the boy's notions of infinity, of how things change but are not destroyed and of how death does not destroy familial bonds, things which had previously unsettled him:

Then I had a strange sensation. It seemed to me that Grandfather's face before me was only a cross section from some infinite stick of rock, from which, at the right point, Mother's face and mine might also be cut. I thought: every face is like this. I had a sudden giddying feeling that there is no end to anything. I wanted to be told simple precise facts. (Section 8)

In the final paragraph of the story, the author returns to the 'existing line' referred to in the first paragraph, a metaphor for familial ties. When the second apparition visits the boy, namely that of the grandfather, he observes: 'He was smiling, and I knew the launch was travelling over to him, unstoppable, unsinkable along that invisible line. And his hands, his acid-marked hands would reach out to receive it'. (Section 11). In essence the boy's father, even in death, provides solace and guidance in an otherwise tumultuous world.

The grandmother

Again, little is known of the grandmother, aside from the fact that she died suddenly and 'inexplicably' when the boy was four. Her death was taken very badly by her husband who demanded more and more time of his daughter. This created tension between the boy's mother and father. Her death, in conjunction with the boy's father's death, united the remainder of the family within a 'sad symmetry' (Section 3) of grief.

Language

Narrative viewpoint

Perhaps the most obvious device used in the story is the narrative viewpoint - the protagonist is also the exclusive author. There are a number of reasons why the boy might represent an unreliable narrator. Firstly, he is reflecting as an adult on a childhood in which he is not party to all the facts. With the passage of time some of his assumptions may have been made concrete in his mind, correctly or incorrectly. We know that his mother never succeeded in explaining the events which unravelled: 'All her life since then... she has been trying to explain, or to avoid explaining...But all the things that should have been explained – or confessed – she never did explain'. (Section 11). Secondly, there is, of course, no additional voice to balance the events described. We know that the boy resents Ralph and has nothing good to say about him - perhaps an additional voice would recount a different story or shine a light on a different man? What the narrative viewpoint does succeed in doing is to allow the reader access to the boy's/man's innermost thoughts and feelings which, in turn, stimulates empathy on the part of the reader.

Foreshadowing

Swift uses foreshadowing to arouse the readers' interest and to steer us toward the conclusion. In Section 1 the grandfather's attempts at salvaging the boat are fruitless. This provides a foreshadowing to the family's eventual demise. The boy describes it as '…the first loss of my life that I had witnessed', the grandfather tells the boy that "You must accept it – you can't get it back – it's the only way." He observes at this stage that his Mother's face is 'very still and very white' as if she 'had seen something appalling'. Again, this is a foreshadowing of revelations to come.

Dialogue & Metaphor

The most significant passage of dialogue (and the longest) takes place in the grandfather's shed between grandfather and grandson. They discuss the science of Chemistry, 'the science of change'. After the grandfather has explained to his grandchild how: "You don't make things in Chemistry – you change them. Anything can change." (Section 7), the boy extrapolates from this a metaphor which he applies to the people in his life. After his grandfather states: "hydrochloric acid and nitric acid. Neither would work by itself, but the mixture will." (Perhaps an oblique reference or metaphor to mother and Ralph – singularly innate but when mixed together - a volatile combination). He asks his grandfather: "People change too, don't they?" (Section 8). To which his grandfather replies: "They change. But the elements don't change. Do you know what an element is? Gold's an element. We turned if from one form into another, but we didn't make any gold – or lose any." Amongst this story's themes are loss and altered family dynamics, the Chemistry metaphor supports these themes.

The boat provides two metaphors – it's trajectory and its 'invisible cord' represent the family's invincible bond (mentioned in Section 1 and Section 11). In Section 1 the boy recounts how the '...voyages were trouble-free'. Then within the parenthesis: 'Then one day – it must have been soon after Mother met Ralph – we watched the boat...the motor cut. The launch wallowed, sank'. In this instance Swift uses the boat's demise to reflect Ralph's destructive impact on the family.

Symbolism and Motif

Swift uses symbolism and motif throughout the story. The motif of water is introduced at the outset: 'The pond in our park was circular…when the wind blew, little waves travelled across it and slapped the paved edges, like a miniature sea'. (Section 1). In this Section water provides a means of uniting the grandfather and boy, who mutually enjoy playing with the boat. However, the water also claims the little boat and later takes on an even more sinister guise when we learn that the sea had claimed the boy's father's life: '…the aircraft disappeared without trace into the Irish Sea…' (Section 3). The apparition of the boy's father in Section 10 appears sodden: '…His hair and clothes were wet, his lips were caked with salt, seaweed hung from his shoulders…Where he trod, pools of water formed on the carpet and slowly oozed outwards…' After the death of the grandfather the boy disposes of the acid, destined for Ralph's face, in the pond (Section 11). Finally, at the conclusion of the story, when the boy feels he has nowhere to go, the pond provides solace and the apparition of the grandfather appears: 'He was smiling, and I knew the launch was still travelling over to him, unstoppable, unsinkable, along that invisible line. And his hands… would reach out to receive it'. (Section 11). The boy's complex relationship with water mirrors the relationship he has with the adults in his life; water, by its very nature, is unstable, shifting, sometimes even perilous.

Swift also uses seasonal changes to highlight different sentiments. In Section 5 when the boy feels that he and his mother are united against Ralph, Swift writes: '…half visible in the twilight, the evergreen shrubs which filled our garden were defying the onset of Autumn'. This is a metaphor for resisting change, namely that of Ralph's involvement with the family. When the grandfather becomes totally isolated, the author writes: 'All that autumn was exceptionally cold. The Evenings were chill and full of rustling leaves…' (Section 9). Here the temperature reflects the iciness of familial relations. Immediately before the boy is informed of his grandfather's death the elements mirror the turbulence to come: 'And then it was almost light and the rain was dashing against the window as if the house were plunging under water…The heavy rain and the tossing branches of the Rowan tree…' (Section 10). Finally, on the day of the grandfather's funeral, the elements reflect the sentiments of the day: 'Grandfather's funeral had been such a day - hard, dazzling, spangled with early frost and gold leaves…'

Alliteration

In *Chemistry* Swift uses alliteration and repetition to emphasize sentiments. In Section 3 he writes: 'For about a year we lived quietly, calmly, even contentedly within the scope of this sad symmetry'. Later he writes: '...and for a whole harmonious year, we were really quite happy'.

Paragraph Structure

Similarly, the author intersperses the story with simple one or two sentence paragraphs to highlight events significant to the narrative:

"The situation was resolved in a dreadful way: by my own father's death." (Section 3); 'But Ralph went pale and rigid and stared at Grandfather without moving'. (Section 4); 'He stared fixedly into my eyes, the way I remembered him doing after Grandmother's death'. (Section 8) and: 'But I must have slept that night, for I do not remember seeing Grandfather's light go out or hearing his steps on the garden path'. This device serves to focus the readers' attention on specific details and creates almost a poetic rhythm to the prose.

Themes

The Living and the Dead - Loss

Perhaps the most obvious theme in this story is that of loss. The boy's father, grandmother and finally grandfather are all losses he has suffered. The grandfather has lost his wife: 'He took his wife's death very badly…' (Section 3) and the mother has lost her husband leaving her: '…in a state which resembled a kind of trance – as if some outside force were all the time directing her…' The narrative describes a boy attempting to rationalize his loss, he considers notions of infinity which, at first, he finds troubling: 'Then I had a strange sensation. It seemed to me that Grandfather's face before me was only a cross Section from some infinite stick of rock, from which, at the right point, Mother's face and mine might also be cut. I thought: every face is like this. I had a sudden giddying feeling that there is no end to anything…' (Section 8). However, after the apparition of both his father and grandfather the boy draws the conclusion, in parallel with the nature of Chemistry which was described to him by his grandfather, that: '…though things change they aren't destroyed"' (Section 11).

The story concludes: 'He (grandfather) was smiling, and I knew the launch was still travelling over to him, unstoppable, unsinkable, along that invisible line…his hands…would reach out to receive it'. In essence the boy's exploration of death and loss delivers to him the notion of life after death, while he has lost his father and grandfather they remain real in his mind and therefore continue to exist in perpetuity.

Family dynamics

'Chemistry' explores family dynamics and how, as with Chemistry itself, altered dynamics can have cataclysmic results. We learn how, after the loss of the grandmother, family relations became strained: 'Grandfather took his wife's death very badly. He needed the company of his daughter and so my father, but he refused to leave the house in which my grandmother had lived, and my parents refused to leave theirs. There was bitterness all around'. (Section 3). The family dynamics shift again when the boy's father dies, which resolved the situation 'in a most dreadful way...' However, with the bitterness gone: 'fate had made him and his daughter quits and reconciled them in mutual grief'. The author speaks of a 'whole harmonious year' in which 'we were really quite happy', he describes an unconventional but ultimately contented family:

We scarcely made any contact with the outside world. Grandfather still worked, though his retirement age had passed, and would not let Mother work. He kept Mother and me as he might have kept his own wife and son...we forgot we were three generations. Grandfather bought Mother bracelets and ear-rings. Mother called me her 'little man'.

The boy isolates the next shift in dynamics with: "Until that day in the park when my boat, setting out across the pond towards Grandfather, sank." (Section 3), which was the 'first loss in my life that I had witnessed'. (Section 1). As we read on we come to understand that the boy is really obliquely referring to the arrival of Ralph. Hostilities quickly surface amongst the family who are returned to a strained existence:

I suppose the question was how far Ralph could tolerate not letting go with Grandfather so as to keep Mother, or how far Mother was prepared to turn against Grandfather so as not to lose Ralph. I remember keeping a sort of equation in my head: if Ralph hurts Grandfather it means I'm right – he doesn't really care about Mother at all; but if Mother is cruel to Grandfather (though she would only be cruel to him because she couldn't forsake him) it means she really loves Ralph (Section 4).

The final shift in family dynamics comes in the form of the Grandfather's death, the boy has lost his ally and is left feeling he has nowhere to go (Section 11).

Loyalty and Betrayal

Loyalty, or allegiance/fidelity all imply a sense of duty or devoted attachment to something or someone. Loyalty connotes sentiment and the feeling of commitment that one holds for one's country, creed, family or friends. At the other end of the scale, the antithesis – namely betrayal, is the breaking or violation of a presumptive contract, trust or confidence that produces moral and psychological conflict within a relationship amongst individuals or organisations. In Section 4 the boy, responding to the mounting conflict within his altered family, reflects on loyalty and perhaps the greatest loyalty shown in the story is that of the boy and his grandfather: they reciprocate allegiance throughout the story. Some would consider his suicide, if it was that, to be a betrayal, but it is never entirely clear how the grandfather met his death. The grandfather remains constant with his daughter but creates conflict and tension both immediately after his wife's death and after the introduction of Ralph. He is 'sour' and 'cantankerous' about the house (Section 7) and he deliberately incites Ralph: 'He deliberately ate slowly to provoke Ralph'. (Section 5). These could be seen as actions synonymous with betrayal of his daughter. However, Ralph is a relative stranger in his home, where: 'Ralph now lorded it, tucking into bigger and bigger meals'. (Section 7). Ralph is rude and abrasive with the elderly grandfather and in his earshot says to the mother: "For Christ's sake we're not waiting up all night for him to finish!" (Section 5).

The mother may also be instrumental in the grandfather's 'betrayal'; she remains passive and neutral, affording her father no defence. The boy describes how his mother has become neglectful of her father in Section 4: '...as Grandfather had pointed out that evening – she would cook the things that Ralph liked (rich thick stews, but not curry) and forget to produce the meals that Grandfather was fond of...' After Ralph's outburst at the table, the grandfather's isolation and extradition to the shed is sealed when the boy's mother suggests: "You're ruining our meal – do you want to take yours out to your shed?!" (Section 5). Remembering that the grandfather has provided for his daughter and grandson, has shown devotion to the boy and given willingly of his time and money, the mother's actions here are clearly a betrayal. She sides with Ralph.

When the mother invites her son to help her collect the dinner plates, she turns to him, gripping his shoulders and asks: 'What am I going to do?' (Section 5). The boy reads this as a desire on his mother's part to return to the 'happy' and 'harmonious' year, prior to Ralph's arrival, described in Section 3: 'She pulled me towards her. I had a feeling of being back in that old impregnable domain which Ralph had not yet penetrated...' (Section 5). However, the mother continues to devote her attentions to her new partner and allows her father to be ostracized. She also allows her son to bear witness to Ralph's detrimental impact on the family, a family in which the mother looks 'trapped and helpless' and where his grandfather '...looked like some torpid, captive animal that had lost even the will to eat'. (Section 9). The boy also observes his grandfather slipping into the house at night 'like a stray cat'. And so the mother's allegiance is clearly exclusively towards Ralph: she affords her child no psychological protection, and in the final paragraphs it becomes clear that her failure to provide an explanation as to the grandfather's death is considered by the boy to be a betrayal. He is left to surmise that his mother's neglect and her lack of loyalty to her father, were probably instrumental in his grandfather's death: '...there was a thousand things I wanted to tell them – about how Mother banished Grandfather, about how suicide can be murder and how things don't end...' (Section 11).

+++++++

The themes referred to above are, of course, not exhaustive. You might want to consider the following alternative themes: Control and Passivity (both Ralph and Grandfather could be seen as controlling characters, whereas the mother and boy are both seemingly passive). Alternately: The Relationship between Adults and Children or the notion of Infinity: 'Things don't end'.

'Odour of Chrysanthemums' – D H Lawrence

Author

David Herbert Lawrence (1885 – 1930) is better known as a novelist. He was born in the coal-mining town of Eastwood near Nottingham and came from a working class background – his father was a coal miner. Lawrence's mother came from a slightly higher class and was unhappy in her marriage to a drunken, feckless miner. Some of Lawrence's fiction – and 'Odour of Chrysanthemums' falls into this category – features a domineering wife with social aspirations, unhappily married to a boorish, loutish working class man.

In adult life, especially after the First World War, Lawrence travelled widely, wrote some acclaimed travel books, and also wrote over 800 poems, most of them in free verse. He also wrote some well-known short stories and several plays. Lawrence believed in spontaneity and naturalness, and many of his poems are about love and relationships: indeed, some of his novels were banned in his lifetime for obscenity. He felt that modern man was insulated by technology and civilization from his true self and from nature. As time has gone on, he is increasingly admired for his short stories and his unflinching yet empathetic portrayal of English working class life – as in 'Odour of Chrysanthemums'. His novels brought him notoriety during his lifetime, but many readers would agree that he is the master of the short story form.

Context

Lawrence wrote the story in 1909 and it was first published in 'The English Review' in July 1911. It was then published in book form in 'The Prussian Officer and Other Stories' on 26th November 1914. Lawrence later turned the story into a play entitled 'The Widowing of Mrs Holroyd'. When Lawrence wrote the story Great Britain was the world's superpower and its Empire covered over a third of the world.

Apart from voyages of discovery and exploration, the driving force behind Britain's pre-eminence had been the Industrial Revolution. From an economic point of view the Industrial Revolution had made the country very wealthy, but it was not such good news for the working classes, forced to work long hours in sometimes dangerous and hazardous conditions. In particular, working conditions for Britain's miners were appalling, and they faced every day the possibility death from suffocation, being crushed by cave-ins and through explosions of underground gas. But coal was necessary to keep the factories supplied with energy; at its height more than a million and a half men worked as coal miners. Lawrence draws carefully on his own experience of working class life which helps give the story an authentic aura. The Industrial Revolution had a huge demographic impact: in 1780 most of the population of Britain lived in the countryside and worked the land; by the time Lawrence is writing most of the population lived in industrial cities or towns and were employed in factories or mines. Although his father never died in a mining accident, Lawrence is writing about a community he knew well.

During the period that this story was written and then published two important social movements were occurring: the suffragette movement which was campaigning to get women the vote and to revolutionize male/female relationships; and the labour movement which through the trades unions and the newly-formed Labour Party sought to improve the lives of the working class. Lawrence has no interest in this story in dealing with these movements at all, preferring to present the problems of Walter and Elizabeth Bates as a more elemental clash of the sexes and of different personalities.

Unfamiliar Words

What follows is a list of formal words of which you may not know the meaning, slang terms used by the mining community in Nottinghamshire, and phonetic spelling of the characters' speech which adds realistic detail.

spinney – a small clump of trees

whimsey – a pit pool formed by any water brought to the surface along with the coal.

pit-bank – a huge mound of earth, rock, coal dust and small pieces of coal, brought to the surface and discarded as unusable rubbish.

sidings – several parallel rows of railway tracks which lead nowhere and are used to 'park' railway engines or wagons that are not in use.

the two wheels… the winding engine – the winding engine is the mechanism that brings cages of miners up to the surface and down to work. Around the two wheels there would have been a thick rope or chain to operate the lift machinery.

winter-crack trees – a type of plum tree with late-ripening plums.

imperious – domineering and powerful.

mien – a look or bearing.

taciturn – silent or not talkative.

wan – pale.

mash – to brew a pot of tea

censure – blame or unfavourable judgment.

Walter's got another bout on – Walter intends to go on a drinking spree.

heered - heard

The Lord Nelson – a local pub.

to spend that b------ afore he went – to spend that bugger (presumably a sum of money) before he left the pub.

A' Saturday night – on Saturday night

It's a settler, it is – Elizabeth's father is praising the tea for settling his stomach.

pertinacity – the quality of being obstinate and stubborn.

Her child chid her… - 'chid' is the past tense of 'to chide; although we would now use 'chided'. If you chide someone you tell them off mildly.

The Prince of Wales – another local pub.

ripping – looking through the pit-bank for small pieces of coal to use on the fire at home.

wafflin' it – waving the piece of bread around aimlessly in front of the fire.

crozzled up – burnt up and singed.

I canna see – I cannot see.

wrath – anger.

sleepers – the huge blocks of wood that railway tracks are laid on.

plaintively – mournfully.

stile – a step for climbing over a wall or fence.

scullery – a room for kitchen work which here doubles as the kitchen itself.

Master – husband.

Mester – phonetic spelling of 'Master'.

childer – dialect word for children.

remonstrance – a strong protest.

I shanna be a minute – I won't be a minute.

Asna 'e come whoam yet? – Hasn't he come home yet?

E's 'appen gone up to th' 'Yew' – The Yew is another local pub.

Ah left him finishing a stint – I left him finishing a piece of work.

Loose-all – the signal for the men to finish work.

Are ter comin', Walt? An' 'e said, 'Go on, Ah shanna be but a 'ef minnit,' so we com'n ter th' bottom, me and Bowers. Thinkin' as 'e wor just behint, an' 'ud come up in the next bantle – Are you coming, Walter? And he said. 'Go on, I won't be half a minute so Bowers and I arrived at the lift. We thought he was just behind us and would come up in the next batch.

Mind!.... Ah've said many a time as Ah'd fill up them ruts in this entry, sumb'dy'll be breaking their legs yit – Be careful! I said many times I would fill up the ruts in this entrance yard or someone will break their legs one day.

I shanna be many minnits. Dunna you be frettin' now' 'e'll be all right – I won't be long. Don't you worry now – he'll be all right.

butty – workmate.

rebuking herself – telling herself off.

peevishly – fretfully and with worry.

vexed – annoyed and troubled.

You mustn't let this upset you, or you know what to expect. How long is it, six months – or is it five? – Elizabeth's mother-in-law is advising her to remain calm or the shock of Walter's accident may bring on a miscarriage and she might lose the baby she is carrying.

''E wor finishing a stint an' th' butties 'ad gone an' a lot o' stuff come down upon him – He was finishing a piece of work and his work-mates had gone and the roof caved in.

… it fell at th' back of him. 'E wor under th' face, an' it never touched 'im. It shut him in. It seems he wor smothered – The cave-in was behind him, so he was not crushed. He was by the coal face and was untouched by the cave-in. But because the cave-in shut him in, he had a limited supply of oxygen and suffocated.

parlour – what we would now call the front room or living room. Used in the past only for very special or out-of-the-ordinary situations.

chiffonier – an ornamental cabinet.

collier – a coal miner.

perplexity – confusion or embarrassment.

'Sphyxiated – asphyxiated, suffocated for want of air to breathe.

countermanded – 'to countermand' literally means to cancel or overturn an order; here it seems that the sight of Walter's dead body has cancelled all her previous feelings about his death.

inviolable – something that can no longer be hurt or distressed.

impregnable – something that cannot be attacked or threatened.

sibilant – hissing.

reparation – to make compensation or amends for some wrong that has occurred.

Plot

The story is written in the third person but is told exclusively from the point of view of Elizabeth Bates, the wife of a miner and mother to John and Annie. She is pregnant with the couple's third child. The story begins with a railway engine pulling seven wagons full of coal. Lawrence is intent in this opening paragraph on presenting the gloomy environment of the pit village and to show the effect of heavy mining on the area. It is dusk and autumn – 'the withered oak leaves dropped noiselessly' – and the railway engine startles a colt while causing a woman to stop walking until the train has passed: she 'stood insignificantly trapped between the jolting black wagons and the hedge'. Lawrence is describing the scene realistically, but he is also using pathetic fallacy: this is going to be a gloomy story and one that revolves around the coal mine. In a long description Lawrence shows how the coal pit has blighted the landscape:

The fields were dreary and forsaken, and in the marshy strip that led to the whimsey, a reedy pit-pond, the fowls had already abandoned their run among the alders, to roost in the tiled fowl-house. The pit-bank loomed up beyond the pond, flames like red sores licking its ashy sides, in the afternoon's stagnant light.

The wheels on the two headstocks are moving, bringing the miners up to the ground at the end of the working day. In the photo above (which is of a Nottinghamshire pit) you can clearly see the winding wheels and the head stocks which support them. The winding wheels operate the lift machinery, bringing cages of miners to the surface. Also on the right of the photo is the pit-bank where coal dust, earth and unusable fragments of coal were piled and any other detritus that was brought to the surface in the process of extracting the coal. Lawrence's description of its 'red sores licking its ashes sides' personifies it and makes it sound thoroughly evil.

Miners start to appear walking to their homes and Lawrence turns the reader's attention to a 'low cottage' and Elizabeth Bates, who is calling her son in because it is getting dark. John, aged 5, has been lurking among the raspberry canes. He is clearly reluctant to come in and as he and his mother walk towards the house 'he tore at the ragged wisps of chrysanthemums and dropped the petals in handfuls along the path' – for which his mother reprimands him, saying it looks "nasty". On impulse she picks a sprig of the flowers and places them in her apron band.

At this point a railway engine pulls up opposite the gate of the house: it is being driven by Elizabeth's father. She takes him a cup of tea and a piece of bread and butter. Elizabeth's father is obviously a widower and tells her rather defensively that he plans to re-marry in order not to be alone as he reaches old age. He is defensive, it seems, because he has not been a widower for long – it is not long since Elizabeth's mother died. He also brings news that Elizabeth's husband, Walter, has been bragging about going on a drinking spree and boasting openly about how much money he will spend in the pub.

Her father drives on and Elizabeth returns to the house, where the table is set for tea. Annie, her daughter, enters and is rebuked mildly by Elizabeth for being late home from school – it now being dark outside. Elizabeth asks Annie if she has seen her father, but she hasn't. At Annie's urging they start the meal without Walter, but Elizabeth eats little and is clearly preoccupied with the thought that her husband is in the pub spending money and not with his family. She listens to the colliery winding gear, but it is silent and she consoles herself with the thought that he may have stopped to do some 'ripping' – searching through the slag heap to find usable pieces of coal.

Elizabeth puts more coal on the fire which makes the room darker and John complains, so Elizabeth lights the central oil lamp. Lawrence uses her action in doing so to reveal that she is pregnant and it also allows Annie to see the sprig of chrysanthemums in her mother's apron band at which she expresses surprise and delight: '"You've got a flower in your apron!" said the child at this unusual event'.

But Elizabeth does not share her daughter's enthusiasm and disagrees that they smell beautiful (in an important quotation we will return to later):

"No." she said, "not to me. It was chrysanthemums when I married him, and chrysanthemums when you were born, and the first time they ever brought him home drunk, he'd got brown chrysanthemums in his button-hole."

As the meal comes to an end, Mrs Bates gives full vent to her anger at her husband:

"Twenty minutes to six!" In a tone of bitter carelessness she continued: "Eh, he'll not come home till they bring him. There he'll stick! But he needn't come rolling in here in his pit-dirt, for I won't wash him. He can lie on the floor – Eh, what a fool I've been, what a fool! And this is what I came here for, to this dirty hole, rats and all, for him to slink past his very door. Twice last week….

The children play quietly for an hour 'united in fear of their mother's wrath, and in dread of their father's home-coming', while the mother sews, keeping her ears open for anyone walking outside.

Then it is time for bed: the children wash and say their prayers, and Elizabeth Bates takes up her sewing again but now – in a foreshadowing of what is to come – '…her anger was tinged with fear'.

Chapter Two of the story begins at eight o'clock that same evening. Elizabeth leaves the house and the children sleeping to find her husband. As she walks to a neighbour's house she berates herself for imagining that 'anything had happened to him'. She calls on Mrs Rigley whose husband has been home for his meal, but has gone briefly to the pub. Mrs Rigley offers to help and fetches her husband from the pub. He says that the last he saw of Walter was in the coal mine finishing a job at the coal face. Mr Rigley kindly offers to check in the other pubs for Walter and walks Mrs Bates home before departing on his errand.

Elizabeth Bates waits for another forty-five minutes when her mother-in-law bursts into the house because she has heard Walter has had an accident in the pit. Elizabeth tries to calm and quieten her, so the children's sleep is not disturbed. A man arrives in pit clothes with the news that Walter is dead – suffocated because of a cave-in close to where he was working which briefly cut him off from the main mine. By the time the other miners had cleared the cave-in Walter had been asphyxiated. Walter's mother wails hysterically but Elizabeth acts calmly, clearing a space in the parlour and laying down a cloth for the body of her husband to be laid upon.

Quite soon the pit manager and a miner arrive with Walter's body on a stretcher. As they bring the body into the parlour they knock over a vase of chrysanthemums on the table, breaking the vase; Elizabeth quickly clears up the mess – typically for Elizabeth, keeping the home as neat and tidy as possible before cleaning her husband's dead body. The commotion downstairs has woken Annie and Elizabeth goes upstairs to quieten her and get her back to sleep, not mentioning Walter's death – that can wait until the morning.

When the men have left the house, Elizabeth and her mother-in-law start to wash and then clothe Walter's body. Lawrence presents Elizabeth reflecting on her marriage to Walter and finally coming to an understanding of it and why it was unsuccessful. Elizabeth even has an epiphany of sorts when she admits to herself that she was partly to blame for the failure of her marriage. This is discussed in greater length below when we consider Elizabeth's character.

Characters

Elizabeth Bates

Lawrence's first description of Elizabeth Bates neatly summarizes her appearance and her character:

She was a tall woman of imperious mien, handsome, with definite black eyebrows. Her smooth black hair was parted exactly.

For most of the story she is angry and bitter at the thought of her husband drinking away precious money in a local pub. Many of her speeches are delivered 'bitterly' and is described by Lawrence as 'bitter'. She seems to feel that she has thrown away all chance of happiness by marrying Walter and she says at one point:

"Eh, what a fool I've been, what a fool! And this is what I came here for, to this dirty hole, rats and all, for him to slink past his very door."

When Annie admires the chrysanthemums tucked in her mother's waistband, Elizabeth calls her 'silly' and removes the flowers 'irritably', before going on to say, in response to Annie's saying that they smell 'beautiful':

"No… not to me. It was chrysanthemums when I married him, and chrysanthemums when you were born, and the first time they ever brought him home drunk, he'd got brown chrysanthemums in his button-hole."

Chrysanthemums play an important role in the story which we examine later.

Elizabeth runs an orderly house and takes pride in the tidiness of the kitchen area. She ensures the children eat, have time to play after the meal, washes them before bed and ensures they say their prayers. However, from what we see in the story she is not very loving and maternal: while they play the children are subdued and do not want to incur their mother's wrath. Nor does she congratulate her father on hearing that he plans to re-marry. She is organized – like her exactly parted hair - but lacks a loving touch perhaps. However, when Walter's mother arrives and later when the mine workers bring Walter's body into the parlour, Elizabeth is very careful that the noise and commotion does not disturb the children's sleep. Annie does wake up when her father's corpse is put in the parlour, but Elizabeth goes up to her and soothes her back to sleep in a gentle and motherly way.

Lawrence is careful to ensure that Elizabeth uses Standard English and not the local accent and she appears to see herself as superior to the rest of the community. For example, she will not demean herself by going into a pub to look for her husband, but is happy for Mrs Rigley to go to the pub to summon her husband; she also views the chaotic untidiness of the Rigley's kitchen with an air of superiority.

However, in the short period of the story when she and her mother-in-law know that Walter had had an accident, but don't know how bad it is, Elizabeth is entirely pragmatic, wondering if he is bed-ridden for a few weeks whether she can stop him drinking altogether, or trying to work out, if he is dead, whether she will be able to manage financially. Her main concern is the children; 'She turned to consider the children. At any rate she was absolutely necessary for them. They were her business'.

But Elizabeth is not devoid of emotion. When confirmation finally comes that Walter has died in the mine 'she wept a little, unknowing' and then remembered that 'they were bringing him home and she must be ready, so she goes and prepares the parlour: significantly there is the 'cold, deathly smell of chrysanthemums in the room'.

Elizabeth and her mother-in-law stand 'arrested in fear and respect' at the sight of Walter naked and they start to clean him. Lawrence writes;

She saw him, how utterly inviolable he lay in himself. She had nothing to do with him. She could not accept it. Stooping down, she laid her hand on him, in claim ....Elizabeth embraced the body of her husband, with cheek and lips. She seemed to be listening, inquiring, trying to get a connection. But she could not. She was driven away. He was impregnable.

Death is the final isolation that awaits us all. As she looks at Walter's body, Elizabeth reflects on her life with him and concludes that he was a stranger to her, just as she was a stranger to him:

There had been nothing between them, and yet they had come together, exchanging their nakedness repeatedly. Each time he had taken her, they had been two isolated beings, far apart as now. He was no more responsible than she.

She seems to accept some responsibility for the failure of their marriage or their unhappiness in it:

…she knew she had never seen him, he had never seen her, they had met in the dark and fought in the dark, not knowing whom they met or whom they fought. And now she saw and turned silent in seeing. For she had been wrong. She had said he was something he was not; she had felt familiar with him. Whereas he was apart all the while, feeling as she never felt.

Lawrence sums up this train of thought by writing "she had refused him as himself". Lawrence also presents Elizabeth as capable of intense emotion and empathy at the close of the story:

… her heart was bursting with grief and pity for him. What had he suffered? What stretch of horror for this helpless man! She was rigid with agony. She had not been able to help him. He had been cruelly injured, this naked man, this other being, and she could make no reparation.

She acknowledges that the children had not helped bring them closer together and, if they were to meet in an after-life, they would be strangers to each other. She ruefully thinks 'how awful' it had been to be a wife, but also recognizes 'how awful he must have felt it to be a husband'. Elizabeth feels 'a terrible dread' and Lawrence writes that 'the horror of the distance between them was almost too much for her' – the distance between life and death, especially given their physical intimacy in life as man and wife.

Lawrence ends the story on a harsh and sombre note:

She knew she submitted to life, which was her immediate master. But from death, her ultimate master, she winced with fear.

Annie Bates

Annie is the seven-year-old daughter of Walter and Elizabeth Bates and is already at school. Lawrence presents her as less self-centred than her brother. She understands why her mother is angry with Walter for going to the pub – she is capable of emotional empathy without once expressing antagonism towards her father. She is old enough to understand that a prolonged bout in the pub by Walter will lead to marital discord.

She is different from her mother, however: she enthuses about the sprig of chrysanthemums that her mother has placed in her apron – an enthusiastic response because it is clear that Elizabeth rarely does such things and she dismisses Annie's rapture over the flowers as 'silly'. While toasting the bread in front of the fire she imaginatively says, "I do think it's beautiful to look in the fire.... It's so red and full of little caves – and it feels so nice and you can fair smell it". Her reaction to the flowers and to the fire show that Annie possesses an enthusiasm for life that her mother has lost.

Annie is woken by the men taking Walter's body into the parlour and shouts down to her mother. Perhaps she has been awake all this time, waiting for her father's arrival – since she understands the implications for family harmony if he rolls back drunk. Elizabeth soothingly placates her and tells her that her father is asleep downstairs. News of the death can wait until the morning.

John Bates

John is the five-year-old son of Walter and Elizabeth Bates. At the start of the story Elizabeth is looking for him, worried that he is near the brook at the bottom of the garden, but, in fact, he is hiding among the raspberry canes. He wears a man's clothes that have been cut down so that they will fit him. Lawrence describes him as 'taciturn' and Elizabeth Bates sees both herself and her husband in her son as he whittles a piece of wood with a knife:

As the mother watched her son's sullen little struggle with the wood, she saw herself in his silence and pertinacity; she saw the father in her child's indifference to all but himself.

In the whole story John remains sullen, speaking only to tell his mother where he is at the start and to complain about the way Annie is toasting the bread before the fire. When the children say their prayers at bed-time, it is typical of John that he mumbles his.

Walter Bates

Although the reader never sees Walter alive in the story, in some ways he is the central character because almost everything in the story revolves around him. Walter is not an alcoholic – alcoholics cannot go for a single day without alcohol – but instead Walter goes on periodic drinking sprees on which he drinks himself into a stupor and has to be carried home – as Elizabeth predicts will happen this evening. From what others say – Elizabeth, Elizabeth's father, Walter's mother – we get the impression that Walter is a feckless, irresponsible drunkard who prefers the pub to the company of his wife and children. However, Walter is not a lazy man – Mr Rigley says Walter stayed at work after the signal to stop work had been given – and working in a coal mine (as Walter's death shows) was an extremely hazardous job: injuries and deaths were common events. We can only guess that Walter's drinking bouts were a reaction to working every day in the pit. When his dead body is brought home, he is naked, innocent and vulnerable, and the sight of him allows Elizabeth to reach a more balanced, more sympathetic view of their marriage acknowledging her role in its failure. We also learn that Walter was a good-looking man, with strong limbs and a moustache. Elizabeth must have been attracted to something in him in order to have married him in the first place, and she is pregnant with their third child, so the marriage was not completely dead.

Walter's Mother

Elizabeth Bates's mother-in-law arrives with the news that Walter has had an accident down the pit. Lawrence uses the mother-in-law in two clear ways: firstly, she is used to build tension because we know that Walter has had an accident but not that he is dead – that news comes later; secondly, Lawrence uses her almost hysterical reaction as a contrast to Elizabeth's more practical and calm approach – Elizabeth is upset and shocked, but not so overt in her emotions. Ever practical, she is already thinking that if Walter is injured and in bed, it will be a good opportunity to wean him from alcohol, and, if he is dead, whether she will be able to manage financially – with a pension from the coal company and her own earnings. The mother-in-law's extrovert weeping and wailing is in clear contrast to Elizabeth's calm and stoical response.

Of course, Walter's mother has known him all his life and can remember him as a child. So she is slightly more indulgent towards his behaviour as an adult. She says:

"Ay – he was a good lad, Elizabeth, he was, in his way. I don't know why he got to be such a trouble, I don't. He was a happy lad at home, only full of spirits. But there's no mistake he's been a handful of trouble, he has! ....You've had a sight of trouble with him, Elizabeth, you have indeed."

Even his own mother recognizes Walter's irresponsible behaviour with money and alcohol.

Mrs Rigley

Mrs Rigley is a neighbour who Elizabeth approaches for help in discovering Walter's whereabouts. She has six children – there are twelve shoes in the kitchen (i.e. six pairs) and Elizabeth notes with disdain and superiority how untidy her kitchen is. Mrs Rigley goes to the pub to fetch her husband, while Elizabeth waits in Mrs Rigley's house in case the children wake up. It is interesting to note that Mrs Rigley is prepared to go inside the pub to fetch her husband – an action Elizabeth sees as beneath her. As soon as Elizabeth leaves with Mr Rigley, his wife rushes next door to spread the gossip about Walter Bates being missing.

Mr Rigley

A fellow miner, Mr Rigley kindly checks the local pubs in an effort to find Walter and discovers that Walter has had an accident – news he passes on to Walter's mother.

Elizabeth's Father

Elizabeth's father is a bearded, cheerful railway engine driver who brings Elizabeth news that he is to re-marry because "It's no sort of life for a man of my years, to sit at my own hearth like a stranger. And if I'm going to marry again it may as well be soon as late – what does it matter to anybody?" He is obviously widowed and slightly concerned that he is marrying too quickly after his first wife's death. Elizabeth does not really reassure him about this, and, although she brings him a cup of tea and a hunk of bread and butter, her attitude to him is quite cold. He apologizes for not coming to see her the previous Sunday, but Elizabeth's reply – "I didn't expect you" – makes him wince. It is Elizabeth's father who first gossips about Walter and tells Elizabeth that Walter had been heard boasting that he would be indulging in a drinking spree that night. Elizabeth's father condemns his actions clearly and sarcastically: "… it's a nice thing when a man can do nothing with his money but make a beast of himself."

Language and Imagery

The dialect and phonetic spelling that Lawrence allows some of the characters to use adds a realistic flavour to the story. It also reveals character because Elizabeth Bates speaks throughout the story in Standard English, showing her social superiority to the community of which she is a part and her aspiration for a better life. Lawrence's use of local dialect and accent does not simply add realism – it increases our sense of Elizabeth's isolation within the mining community.

Lawrence's own writing is precise and he makes frequent use of simile and metaphor. His opening description of the mining community (which is examined in more detail below under Setting) shows the coal mine and its environment having a negative effect on nature and on the humans who have the misfortune to live and work there. Apart from the pollution coming from the coal mine, the human beings in the landscape are threatened too: the raspberry canes from which John emerges are 'like whips'. It is almost as if the humans in the story are about to disappear: the miners walk home 'like shadows' and later in the story Elizabeth puts a dustpan outside and returns to the house 'like a shadow'.

The animal and natural imagery that Lawrence uses suggests very broadly that the characters are part are of a larger and very unpredictable cycle of life and death. John is compared to a frog when he crawls out from beneath the sofa' Elizabeth predicts that when his mates carry Walter home drunk he will be 'like a log'. Walter, according to one of the miners who carries the stretcher with Walter's corpse on it, says he was caught like a mouse in a mouse trap – a simile that might apply to all the families and miners forced to live in the pit village.

Walter's mother's tears are like 'drops from wet leaves' – Lawrence suggests she is weeping so copiously because she thinks it is expected of her. The unborn child is 'like ice' in Elizabeth as the truth of Walter's death hits her and the financial difficulties she will face become apparent. At critical points in the story – firstly out of anger at Walter and then out of dread and fear – Elizabeth's heart seizes up and fills with tension. Finally in the last sentence of the story, life and death are personified as Elizabeth's two masters.

At the same time, perhaps because he is writing about a milieu he knows so well, Lawrence writes a convincingly realistic story about working class life from the efforts to keep the fire going, the simple, filling meal, the rats in the yard and the single candle which illuminates the laying out of Walter's corpse at the end of the story.

Lawrence's use of dialogue is also very succinct: he manages to convey a lot of information through small breaks of dialogue: the miners who bring the corpse are sympathetic but fairly taciturn because there is nothing they can say which might console Elizabeth. The longest speeches are by Elizabeth when she is complaining to the children about Walter's behaviour, and Walter's mother when she is remembering what Walter was like as a child.

Finally Lawrence's description of Elizabeth's highly complex feelings are dealt with superbly by Lawrence's analytical prose. He leads us as readers to Elizabeth's epiphany and her realization that she was partly responsible for never accepting or truly knowing the man that Walter was. This realization comes to Elizabeth slowly and incrementally, and Lawrence's prose guides the reader adeptly through her tumultuous feelings and thoughts.

Prolepsis and Foreshadowing

Lawrence uses both prolepsis and foreshadowing in the story and, while the techniques are similar, they are not the same at all. Foreshadowing is a moment in the story when a character says or thinks something that will come true later in the story or which hints at something which will come true. For example, at the end of the first chapter Lawrence writes of Elizabeth, 'Meantime her anger was tinged with fear' – anger that Walter is drinking in the pub tempered by fear that he has had an accident in the mine.

On the other hand, prolepsis is a form of irony – proleptic irony. This works in the following way: something happens or something is said which turns out to be ironic in the light of later events. On several occasions Elizabeth talks about how his mates will have to carry him home from the pub dead drunk and she states that he can sleep on the floor where they drop him: these are examples of prolepsis because they are ironically wrong as we read the rest of the story, because, although Walter is carried home and left on the parlour floor, he is dead, suffocated in the mine. The following quotation from Elizabeth is a perfect example of prolepsis:

"Twenty minutes to six! ….eh, he'll not come now till they bring him. There he'll stick! But he needn't come rolling in here in his pit-dirt, for I won't wash him. He can lie on the floor."

And a little later, "They'll bring him when he does come – like a log". The irony lies in the partial truth of Elizabeth's words – they do carry him into the parlour and, in fact, she does end up washing him because he is dead. It is irony because she is wrong and proleptic irony because we only recognize it in hindsight as we look back over the story or read it for a second time.

Setting

The setting of 'Odour of Chrysanthemums' is bleak and bare. In his opening paragraph Lawrence shows the clash between the mechanized world of the mine and the natural world. The railway engine startles a colt and forces a young woman to get out of its way and shelter next to a hedge. The pit-bank is described as having 'flames like red sores licking its ashy sides' making it sound like a wounded beast. The fields are 'dreary and forsaken'. The oak is 'withered', the cabbages are 'ragged', the chrysanthemums are 'dishevelled' and even Elizabeth's son is lost in the darkness. The miners trooping homewards are 'shadows'. Nature seems to be hostile to humanity: the Bates's cottage is - 'A large bony vine clutched at the house, as if to claw down the tiled roof'. The Bates's house is small with a kitchen where they eat, live and play, and a front room or parlour which is used for special occasions – such as the laying out of a dead body. Presumably there are two bedrooms upstairs. The yard is infested with rats. The Bates are poor which makes Walter's wasting money on beer even more foolhardy. Most of the story takes place in darkness because it is late afternoon and twilight when the story begins and ten o' clock at night when the men bring Walter's body to the house. The darkness also reflects the tragic outcome of the story and the hard lives that the characters face in the pit village.

Themes

Poverty

The Bates are a poor family: working class workers were paid very badly during this era and trade unionism was in its relative infancy, so the workers found it hard to negotiate for better pay: however, Lawrence has no interest in this side of his story. The poverty of the family is clear and must add to the strains in the marriage when Walter wastes so much money in the pub. Signs of poverty are John's clothes:

some of Walter's old clothes cut down to fit his five-year-old frame. The children's evening meal consists of large pieces of toasted bread – cheap but filling, followed by batter pudding – another cheap but filling dish. The cottage they live in is small and has no electricity – light comes from candles, the fire and oil lamps – one of which Elizabeth lights in the course of the meal. In the garden there are signs that they grow their own vegetables to save money – the cabbages and the raspberry canes – and they keep chickens in a fowl house – for eggs and meat.

Conflict and Divisions

Throughout the story Lawrence presents aspects of life or areas of life which are in conflict with each other, and these dichotomies centre around his thematic concerns.

One conflict is between man and his environment which we have touched on in writing about setting. The bleak environment of the pit village is presented as hostile to man and to nature, and also disrupts the human relationship with nature. The miners trooping homeward are mere 'shadows' and their lives are blighted by the coal mine; Walter's death in the mine could be seen as symbolic of the way the mine dominates and pollutes the landscape. Working in the coal mine is dangerous, dirty and physically-exhausting work with the constant threat of injury or death. Nature too is ruined by the demands of industrialized society as Lawrence's opening description shows so vividly.

Lawrence presents an element of social class conflict too in Elizabeth's sense of her own superiority to her neighbours. Ironically the neighbours Elizabeth looks down on are warm, friendly people who gladly give up their time to help Elizabeth in her search for Walter. But we might note that Mrs Rigley speaks to Elizabeth 'in a tone tinged with respect'. Elizabeth is still working class, but she seems aspirational and resents living where she does – 'this dirty hole' – and we can see that she is trying to bring up John and Annie with a sense of decorum and good behaviour.

The conflict between men and women is epitomized in the Bates's marriage, and it was a conflict that Lawrence often returned to in his novels and other stories. For most of the story we are encouraged, by Lawrence's narrative point of view, to see Walter as the problem – wasting his wages in prolonged drinking sessions and neglecting his wife and children as he does so. Indeed, Elizabeth could be said to be suffocating in her marriage to Walter, although Lawrence never uses any imagery to suggest that. However, the end of the story leads to Elizabeth's insight that she is as much to blame for any failings in their marriage as Walter was. They have produced three children but – despite the physical intimacy that involved – they were strangers to each other:

There had been nothing between them, and yet they had come together, exchanging their nakedness repeatedly. Each time he had taken her, they had been two isolated beings, far apart as now.... And her soul died in her for fear: she knew she had never seen him, he had never seen her, they had met in the dark and fought in the dark, not knowing whom they met nor whom they fought.

Elizabeth's epiphany allows her to see that she was partly to blame for the failings in her marriage: 'She had denied him what he was – she saw it now. She had refused him as herself – she saw it now'. Most of Lawrence's novels deal with relationships between men and women, and one phrase from the last quotation above stands out – 'in the dark' – Lawrence could justifiably be said to be in favour of greater openness and light in dealing with sexual and emotional matters between men and women. This understanding leads to empathy on Elizabeth's part, but also an awareness that they are now separated for ever by death. And so the story ends with a major division – that between the living and the dead.

Most of the story takes place in the dark, but Lawrence uses light as a contrast throughout the story. The light in the kitchen comes from the fire until Elizabeth lights the central oil lamp. The family eat their meal with their faces in darkness – John 'was almost lost in darkness' and his face is 'a dusty mark on the shadow'. By contrast, the Prince of Wales pub looks 'warm and bright'. John often complains about the room being too dark, and we learn he is like his father in this respect, while Annie is transfixed by the brightness and colour of the fire itself. However, fire carries a potential danger – while Mrs Rigley goes to get her husband from the pub she asks Elizabeth to wait for her to ensure that "th' childer doesn't come downstairs and set theirselves afire." In a story that revolves around a death, Lawrence uses light and dark to foreshadow in a very general way Walter's passage to the ultimate darkness – death.

The contrast between the living and the dead is also central to the story. In practical terms – a widow with three children to bring up – Walter's death is a disaster for the family. In addition, Elizabeth is astonished at the transformation that death brings: as they attempt to clothe Walter's corpse at the end of the story

He was so heavy and inert. A terrible dread ripped her all the while: that he could be so heavy and utterly inert, unresponsive, apart. The horror of the distance between them was almost too much for her – it was so infinite a gap she must look across.

However, in terms of what Elizabeth learns about her marriage (albeit in retrospect) and what the readers perceive about the awful finality of death, the whole story could be said to be building up to the final sentence:

She knew she submitted to life, which was her immediate master. But from death, her ultimate master, she winced with fear and shame.

To submit to something means to surrender and Elizabeth is caught as effectively as Walter is in the mining accident – "like a mouse-trap" – because she has two, soon to be three, children to bring up, but her submission to life means that she is willing to face up to her responsibilities.

The Motif of Chrysanthemums

Apart from being in the title, chrysanthemums recur throughout the short story. Chrysanthemums come in thousands of varieties and are valued for the variety of their petal structure and the bright, vivid nature of their blooms, particularly as they bloom in late summer and the autumn. Their scent is more variable and some chrysanthemums have a musty, pungent almost acrid smell. In most European countries chrysanthemums are associated with funerals and, therefore, death.

John scatters chrysanthemum petals across the path at the start of the story and is reprimanded by his mother because it looks nasty; Elizabeth places a sprig of chrysanthemums in her apron band which Elizabeth enthuses over – although she is told she is being 'silly' by her mother and Elizabeth bursts out bitterly when Annie says they smell beautiful:

"No." she said, "not to me. It was chrysanthemums when I married him, and chrysanthemums when you were born, and the first time they ever brought him home drunk, he'd got brown chrysanthemums in his button-hole."

Later in the story when the men carry Walter's body into the parlour one of the men knocks over a vase of chrysanthemums on the table breaking the vase – it is almost a symbolic gesture summing up the tragedy of Walter's death, the Bates's unhappy marriage and the difficult and poverty-stricken life that Elizabeth can look forward to as a widow with three children under ten.

The Ending

There is no doubt that faced with Walter's naked body and engaged in the act of washing it, Elizabeth comes to realize how little she knew her husband, how little they knew each other and that if their marriage was a failure it was the fault of both of them. She is also overawed by the enormity and finality of death, knowing that she must live on in order to look after the children. Some readers have suggested that the final scene in the parlour resembles the paintings in the pietà tradition: paintings depicting Jesus being washed by his mother and Mary Magdelene after his death on the cross (like the one above). We are not sure Lawrence intended this, and it certainly does not transform Walter into a Christ-like figure, but it does make clear his role as innocent victim – a victim (like the landscape) of industrialization and mechanization.

'My Polish Teacher's Tie' – Helen Dunmore

Author

Helen Dunmore was born in 1952 in Yorkshire. She was the second of four children and her father was the eldest of twelve; she attributes being part of a large family as instrumental to her prolific writing career. Amongst her various credentials she won the inaugural Orange Prize for Fiction in 1996, a prize awarded specifically to female writers, with her third novel *A Spell of Winter.*

'My Polish Teacher's Tie' is one of 18 short stories extracted from her book *Ice Cream. Ice Cream* was also nominated for the Orange Prize in 2003.

The author's recurrent themes consist of love and loss, food and landscapes.

Plot

'My Polish Teacher's Tie' is set in a school canteen and its protagonist (the leading character) is a school dinner lady, Carla Carter. It is written in the first person. In the fourth paragraph Carla reveals that she is half Polish, although she does not speak the language. Her English father objected to Carla speaking Polish with her mother, believing that it would confuse his child.

At the weekly staff meeting the Head announces plans to arrange a teacher exchange. We are told that several Polish teachers are looking for pen friends in English schools (to improve their written English). Carla volunteers and begins corresponding with Stefan, or Steve as he prefers to be known. Carla harbours a nagging guilt, knowing that Steve believes he is communicating with another teacher, not a school dinner lady.

Through their correspondence Carla's love of poetry is rekindled and her hunger to learn more of her Polish heritage exposed. Steve's letters provide her with a great source of pleasure and the frequency of their exchanges begins to increase.

After what we can assume have been several weeks the Head announces that a teacher will be visiting from Poland on exchange. That teacher is Steve. Carla is mortified, knowing that Steve will discover her real identity. Their correspondence ceases after Carla receives a letter from Steve, confirming his exchange visit. She thinks the tone is polite but cooler and she concludes that Steve feels rejected, having assumed her to be a teacher and aware of his imminent arrival, but having not volunteered to play host. She considers her options, including taking time off sick, but eventually persuades herself to stop worrying.

After Steve's arrival at the school and before Carla has met him she overhears a conversation between two teachers. Valerie Kenwood, who is playing host to Steve, speaks of him in a disparaging manner, criticizing his accent, his clothes (particularly his ties) and his preoccupation with literature. Carla then spots Steve in the canteen and summons up the courage to approach him, despite her feelings of guilt and inadequacy.

Steve, who is delighted to meet Carla contrary to her expectations, breaks into song. It is a song that Carla finally recognises from her early childhood. The story closes with the two of them singing in faltering duet much to the surprise of the Head.

Characters

Carla Carter

Although not mentioned in the story, we can assume from the omissions that Carla is a single parent, mother to only-child Jade. She describes herself in the first paragraph as 'part-time catering staff, that's me £3.89 per hour'. She is someone who is focused on her perceived standing in society and refers to herself continually in a self-deprecating fashion. Carla is a quiet woman but acutely conscious of her surroundings and her inner-monologue demonstrates a highly observant and empathetic nature. On occasions she can be sarcastic, scathing and quite child-like.

Stefan (Steve) Jeziorny

Steve is a polite young Polish teacher with a passion for literature and poetry. He is someone who enjoys sharing his passion as indicated by the contents of his letters to Carla. He is portrayed as a driven man with a humorous and optimistic outlook on life.

The scenes in the canteen reveal that he is not a judgmental person and that he too lacks confidence and self-esteem.

The Head

The Head is presented through Carla's narrative as a bumbling man, lacking in sincerity and with little knowledge of his staff outside the teaching fraternity.

Valerie Kenward

Valerie, Steve's host and a teacher at the school, is portrayed as a smug, greedy, highly critical woman, lacking in empathy. Her children appear to have inherited some of her worst traits. She is not someone to reason with and voices her opinions in a bullish way. Both she and the Head represent the anti-hero to the characters of Carla and Steve.

Language

The language used throughout the story is simple and colloquial. Sentences are short and contractions used throughout: 'Somebody'd remember me.....' This gives the story a very chatty and intimate feel. Steve's language, meanwhile, demonstrates that whilst his English is highly competent, it lacks the fluidity of native speakers: 'You will know from your school, Carla, that I will come to England'. Whilst it makes perfect grammatical sense, we would write: 'that I will be coming to England'.

Carla's use of language changes dramatically on meeting Steve. She begins to introduce similes: 'He was tense as a guitar string' and 'It went through me like a knife through butter'. She also uses alliteration: 'His big bright tie blazing'.

The use of these poetic devices suggests an awakening in Carla, a determination to put aside her sense of inadequacy and to embrace her love of poetry.

Themes

Taken at its most literal and simplistic level, 'My Polish Teacher's Tie' describes how a school dinner lady rises above her personal inadequacies to explore her past and broaden her horizons. Steve provides the role of catalyst. A kind of alchemy ensues, arising from the collision of two worlds.

Sense of Self-worth

The theme of self-worth runs through the core of the story. Carla's self-worth or, rather, lack of it, is demonstrated by her acute awareness of her perceived social standing. In line 100 she identifies herself as being a separate entity from the teaching staff: 'Colleagues don't wear blue overalls and white caps and work for £3.89 an hour'. Similarly, on line 25 Carla recounts how 'the meeting broke up and the Head vanished in a knot of teachers.....' The use of the word 'knot' in describing the collective of teachers again suggests that Carla perceives herself as an outsider and that the collective, the 'knot', is impenetrable. In line 27 she observes that 'teachers are used to getting out of the way of catering staff without really seeing them'. She feels invisible.

Her opinions on the teaching staff are made clear by her omission in the opening paragraph: 'I dish out tea and buns to the teachers twice a day, and I shovel chips on the kids' trays at dinner-time. It's not a bad job. I like the kids'. She 'likes' the kids but makes no such comment on the teachers.

In line 22 she takes ownership of her lesser role: 'I wrung out a cloth and wiped my surfaces', as if to say 'I know my place'. And in line 29, in trying to get the Head's attention she repeats "excuse me" three times, which serves to stress her invisibility. When the Head finally notices Carla, she recounts how he 'stitched a smile on his face', suggesting that Carla finds him insincere and reluctant to engage with her. He then stumbles over her name and assumes that whatever she wants it means trouble: "Oh, er - Mrs, er – Carter. Is there a problem?" The hesitation in identifying Carla by name acts to highlight her sense of inferiority.

Similarly, in her relationship with Steve, she feels that without hanging on to the pretence of being a teacher he will become instantly disinterested, drawing her assumption from the attitude of the teaching staff around her. In line 106, having just been made aware of Steve's impending visit, she ruminates: 'He'd think I was trying to make a fool of him, making him believe I was a teacher. Me, Carla Carter, part-time catering assistant, writing to him about poetry'. (line 121-122).

Steve qualifies her interest in poetry; without him she feels unworthy to pursue her interest alone: 'And then there was the poetry book I'd bought. It seemed a shame to bin it. It might come in use for Jade, I thought'.

Loss and Retrieval of Identity

We learn that Carla is half-Polish very early on in the story. Her mother used to read rhymes to her, until her English father objected to her speaking Polish. She recounts her father's rationale in line 15: "You'll get her all mixed up, now she's going to school. What use is Polish ever going to be to her?" In line 13 she conveys how detached she feels from her Polish heritage: 'I'm half-Polish. They don't know that here. My name's not Polish or anything...I spoke Polish till I was six, baby Polish.....' Later in the paragraph she admits she recalls nothing of the language: 'I can't speak it now. I've got a tape, a tape of me speaking Polish with Mum. I listen, and think I'm going to understand what we're saying, and then I don't'.

Through her correspondence with Steve, she slowly retrieves some of her lost language and heritage but she also begins to identify herself as something beyond just a dinner lady. When they eventually meet in line 154 the layout of the dialogue breaks from convention: "Hello', I said. He jumped up, held out his hand. 'How do you do?' he asked....' Here both of them speak on the same line, which is entirely unique within the body of the story. Sharing the line evokes a sense of shared identity, a unification of two lonely souls.

The story closes with Steve breaking into song. It is a song that Carla recognizes and she joins in. She is finally reunited with her past. With a renewed sense of self, she allows herself to be defined by who she is rather than what she does. The Head, astounded by the singing says: "Good heavens. How very remarkable. I didn't realize you were Polish, Mrs... er..." To which Carla replies: "Nor did I." The sentence continues with Carla's inner monologue: 'But I wasn't going to waste time on the Head. I wanted to talk about poetry. I smiled at Steve'.

The Imperialist Legacy

Valerie Kenward's scathing attitude towards Steve and her outspoken ridicule of his accent, clothing and conversation are all suggestive of a deeply entrenched sense of British superiority. Carla describes how 'the Head was wagging a sheaf of papers in front of him (Steve), talking very loudly, as if he were deaf'. This again indicates that Steve is perceived to be a lesser being. The theme is also touched upon in line 15 where Carla's English father dismisses the value of the Polish language and perhaps his daughter: 'What use is Polish going to be to her?'. The contempt shown towards Poland and Steve himself could be attributed to imperialism's legacy – an unspoken but continuing sense of national supremacy and prejudice.

Hope

Steve's garish tie symbolizes a beacon of hope, both for himself and Carla, it could be seen to represent a breaking down of prejudice and social judgement. Both find themselves on the receiving end of discrimination. A particularly good example for Carla is when she requests the Polish teacher's address in line 33 and the Head fails to see her as a potential pen friend: "I was just wondering, could I have that address?' 'Address?' 'The Polish one. You said there was a Polish teacher who wanted an English penfriend'. 'Oh. Ah, yes'. He paused, looking at me as if it might be a trick question."

Valerie Kenward provides the voice of discrimination in Steve's case

Carla acknowledges Steve's slightly unusual appearance: 'He was wearing a brown suit with padded shoulders. It looked too big for him. His tie was wider than normal ties, and it was red with bold green squiggles on it. It was a terribly hopeful tie'. Notice how Carla herself associates the tie with hope.

The final paragraph is symbolic of the breaking down of prejudice, Steve has accepted Carla for what she is, not what she does and the tie becomes a metaphor for a world without discrimination, a world with hope:

His red tie with its bold green squiggles was much too wide and much too bright. It was a flag from another country, a better country than the ones either of us lived in 'I like your tie,' I said.

A Note on Ownership

The title of the book suggests that the protagonist is a school child. The first line of the story is also indicative of this: 'I wear a uniform, blue overall and white cap with the school logo'. However, we quickly learn that Carla is a school dinner lady. The use of 'My' in the title suggests a sense of ownership. Later in the story Steve will address Carla with: "Carla! You are Carla Carter. My penfriend." This language of ownership acts to highlight the bond between the two individuals who, aside from their own mutual relationship, appear lost and unconnected to any social grouping.

A Note on Steve's First Poem

The first poem Steve sends to Carla describes a bird in a coal mine. It becomes trapped but continues singing until it eventually dies. Everyone can hear it singing, but no one can find it. Traditionally canaries were used as a warning system for toxic levels of carbon monoxide and methane. If the bird died it gave the miners sufficient time to exit the mine before they too were poisoned. In a sense Steve could be seen to represent the bird he describes. He has three things in common with the creature, he is in a foreign environment, he feels lost and yet despite this in the final paragraphs he breaks into song. Steve, therefore, could be seen to represent Carla's canary, protecting her from her own poison – low self-esteem and a sense of not belonging.

'Korea' – John McGahern

Author

John McGahern (12 November 1934 – 30 March 2006) is regarded as one of the most important Irish writers of the latter half of the twentieth century. Known for the intrinsic and precise dissection of Irish life found in works such as *The Barracks*, *The Dark* and *Amongst Women*, *The Observer* hailed him as "the greatest living Irish novelist" before his death in 2006. His short stories have also received high praise and popularity.

John McGahern's writing career was plagued by controversy due to his challenging many of Ireland's past religious, social, and sexual values. His novel *The Dark* was banned in 1965 in the Irish Republic for obscenity. Although such abstract social issues are not at the centre of his stories, there are no sentimental images of Ireland in them either; many are darkly pessimistic or bleakly realistic.

Context

The Irish War of Independence or Anglo-Irish War was a guerrilla war fought from 1919 to 1921 between the Irish Republican Army (the army of the Irish Republic) and the British security forces in Ireland. It was an escalation of the Irish revolutionary period into warfare. A peace treaty was signed in July 1921 to bring an end to the conflict and British troops withdrew from Ireland. In 1922 the Irish Free State was established, leaving Great Britain with no authority over Ireland except in the six counties that form Ulster or Northern Ireland – which to this day remains part of the United Kingdom.

Mountjoy Prison – the main prison in Dublin. Many Irish Republicans were interned in the prison by the British Army during the Irish War of Independence and many were executed there.

The Korean War (25 June 1950 – 27 July 1953) was a war between North and South Korea, in which a United Nations force led by the United States of America fought for the South, and China fought for the North, which was also assisted by the Soviet Union. The war arose from the division of Korea at the end of World War II and from the global tensions of the Cold War that developed immediately afterwards.

There is a long tradition of Irish people emigrating from Ireland in search of a better life. The Irish diaspora refers to Irish people and their descendants who live outside Ireland. Since 1700 between 9 and 10 million people born in Ireland have emigrated. This is more than the population of Ireland at its historical peak in the 1830s of 8.5 million. The poorest of them went to Great Britain, especially Liverpool; those who could afford it, almost 5 million, went to the United States. After 1840, emigration from Ireland became a massive, relentless, and efficiently managed national enterprise. In 1890 40% of Irish-born people were living abroad. By the 21st century, an estimated 80 million people worldwide claimed some Irish descent; which includes more than 36 million Americans who claim Irish as their primary ethnicity.

Plot

The significance of the title does not become clear until late on in the story – and it is also probably a pun on 'Career'. The story too seems very simple: a father and son are performing for the last time their daily activities to do with catching eels in the estuary of an Irish river. In the morning they collect the eels that have been caught and send them off to Billingsgate, the London fish market once a week; in the evening they bait the lines ready for the night's catch. The father also grows potatoes for a living.

However, buried in the narrative of 'Korea' are two other stories which alter the meaning and impact of 'Korea' and will be discussed fully in the commentary. The first concerns a memory the father has of being a prisoner of the British in Mountjoy Prison during the Irish War of Independence. He recalls watching as the British executed two Irish prisoners in the prison courtyard and it is a memory that has remained vivid in his mind since then. The second story concerns a local boy, Luke Moran, who had emigrated to America and joined the American army; Luke's family had received $250 a month while he was in the US army and $10,000 when he died. In addition, he was given a full military burial back home in Ireland. The son overhears his father talking about this with a cattle dealer called Farrell. This is significant only because during their morning work on the river, the father had encouraged his son to consider emigrating to America, even offering to scrape together the money for the fare there. On the river that evening the father asks his son if he had decided whether to go to America or not, and the son replies that he has decided not to go.

This summary sounds as if a greedy father is trying to manipulate his son in order to gain financially. Growing potatoes brings in little money and, with his son gone, he will have to pay someone to row the boat while he baits the eel-lines or collects the catch. There is also some doubt about whether the local council will renew his fishing licence – they would rather attract English tourist fishermen to the area. However, the son reacts positively to his father, firmly tells him that he will not be going to America and, despite what appears to be his father's attempted manipulation of him for money, states at the end of the story that he had never felt closer to his father than he did at that moment.

Commentary

'Korea' is written in the first person from the point of view of the unnamed son, looking back on the events of one day from some point years in the future. The story is set in the early 1950s while the war in

Korea was going on. The opening sentence "You saw an execution then too, didn't you?" plunges us straight back into Ireland's violent past – specifically the Irish War of Independence. McGahern relates the story to begin with in reported speech. The full opening sentence is even more important:

"You saw an execution then too, didn't you?" I asked my father, and he started to tell as he rowed.

This sentence contains all the crucial elements of the story: the father and son working together; one of them asking a question – these elements will be repeated throughout the story. The reported narration suggests that the son has heard the story before and therefore can repeat it in reported speech – the son's "didn't you?" implies as much. He is asking a question about a war while another war – the one in Korea – is going on.

While imprisoned in Mountjoy by the British the father has seen, from his cell window, two Irish republican prisoners executed. They are being executed simply as a reprisal for a Republican attack unconnected with these two particular men. One is young – perhaps close to the son's own age – and is weeping as he is led to the execution spot: he accepts the blindfold and stands to attention when ordered to do so by the British officer. The older prisoner refuses the blindfold and stands with his hands nonchalantly in his pockets, ignoring the officer's command to take his hands out of his pockets. The two men die very differently too: the older man simply falls backwards, but the younger man desperately tears at his tunic as the bullets strike his chest and the metal buttons of his uniform fly off 'before he pitched forward on his face'. In their two different reactions we see innocence and experience at work: the younger man 'clicked to attention' when told to and continues to fight by tearing at his tunic as the bullets hit; the older man is more casual and laid-back – eyes wide open, hands in pockets, chewing silently. To explain the different directions they fell there is the ironic comment on the older man – 'it must have been because his hands were in his pockets'. After thc firing squad have killed the two men, the British officer, with his revolver, fires one bullet into the young man to ensure that he is dead, but 'he pumped five bullets in rapid succession into the [older] man, as if to pay him back for not coming to attention'. This may assuage the British officer's anger. but it is meaningless and completely futile since the man is already dead.

The focus of the story now shifts to the way that the memory of that scene has haunted the father over the years. The father speaks of his honeymoon "years later" and describes a memorable scene:

"The sea was below, the smell of the sea and furze-blossom all about, and then I looked down and saw the furze pods bursting, and the way they burst in all directions seemed shocking like the buttons when he started to tear at his tunic. I couldn't get it out of my mind all day. It destroyed the day."

Later the father makes it clear that the memory destroyed more than that one day on his honeymoon. He is still haunted and moved by the executions he witnessed over thirty years before and the memory has the ability to taint, with warfare and reprisal executions, the idyllic rural landscape of Ireland.

The son-narrator asks "Do you think the boy stood to attention because he felt he might still get off if he obeyed the rules?" But the father – in the first sign of conflict between him and his son – dismisses the notion as innocent and pretentious, saying,

"Sounds a bit high-falutin' to me. Comes from going to school too long," he said aggressively, and I was silent. It was new to me to hear him talk about his own life at all. Before, if I asked him about the war, he'd draw his fingers across his eyes, as

if to tear a spider's web away, but it was my last summer with him on the river, and it seemed to make him want to talk, to give of himself before it ended.

We might note that McGahern again uses a simile from nature (the spider's web) when writing about the war (like the furze pods exploding), and are we to detect a hint of resentment at career choices available to the son but denied the father in the "going to school too long"?

The next two paragraphs describe the work the son is doing in taking the eels into the boat. The father and son work in harmony together which creates a placid, contemplative mood as McGahern describes the details of work they have done together many times in the past. The son works efficiently, methodically and McGahern makes the process sound like a well-practised ritual, given greater poignancy since we now know this is the last summer the son will spend on the river doing this job. 'We were the last to fish this freshwater for a living' – the work the father and son do is one that will die when they stop doing it.

After a mile they swap roles so that the son rows, and the father deals with the eels. It is also the father's turn to ask questions about the son's plans for the future. It is clear that the son is waiting for the results of his examinations, which implies that he is eighteen, and the results of the exams will determine what profession he enters or even (though it is not mentioned) take up a place at university. The son says that if the results are good then he will have "choices" and seems to think the results will be "all right, but there's no counting chickens, is there?"

At this point there is another change of tone. The father's reaction is interesting: he replies "No"' he said, but there was *something calculating* [my italics] in his face; it made me watchful of him as I rowed the last stretch of the line." "Something calculating" is a strikingly vague phrase in a story so rich in detail – and it stands out as a result. They continue with their work, the father remarking that "'We'll have enough [eels] for a consignment tomorrow." Each week we sent the live eels to

Billingsgate in London'. But the son makes no reply, bringing a moment of awkward silence to the story.

The father then makes a long speech: "But say, say even if you do well, you wouldn't think of throwing this country up altogether and going to America?" The repeated "say" and the beginning with "but" show the father's nervousness in bringing up this question. When the son asks why go to America the father makes a long speech:

"Well, it's the land of opportunity, isn't it, a big expanding country? There's no room for ambition in this poky place. All there's room for is to make holes in pints of porter."

But the son remains wary and comments 'I was wary of the big words. They were not in his voice'. At this stage neither father nor son are saying what they really want to say – as becomes clear later in the story. The father insists that somehow they will scrape together enough money for the son's fare to America. The son maintains his wariness in the questions he asks, wary and caught off guard by his father's unexpected suggestion. When the son asks "Why should you scrape for me to go to America when I can get a job here?" The father replies:

"I feel I'd be giving you a chance I never got. I fought for this country. And now they want to take away the licence to fish. Will you think about it anyhow?"

The son promises to think about it. The father's frustration at fighting for his country to be free of English rule is clear. He fought to preserve a way of life that is now under threat. He is facing new economic realities which he cannot control, but which are determined by England: the live eels are sold to the London fish market, and the last time he went to renew his fishing licence, the local tourist board had opposed his application:

They said we impoverished the coarse fishing for tourists – the tourists who came every summer from Liverpool and Birmingham in increasing numbers to sit in aluminium deck-chairs on the river bank and fish with rods.

Father and son set about their daily tasks and are separate for the first time in the story. The father is working in the potato fields; the son re-hooks the lines and digs up worms to be used as bait.

Partly because the son is doing this for the last time he reflects on what he is doing and gives the reader an insight into how he feels. For the first time in the story we get a detailed insight into the narrator's thoughts. He feels a pain

…of doing things for the last time as well as the boredom the knowledge brings that soon there'll be no need to do them, that they could be discarded almost now. The guilt of leaving came: I was discarding his life to assume my own.

It is vital to note and remember the son's strong feeling of guilt: he is leaving his father in an impoverished position with a paltry income from his potatoes and the cost of employing a man to share the eel-catching activities – that is, if his fishing licence is granted.

The climax of the story takes us by surprise – just as it shocks the son. The son is taking the worms to the lavatory where they store them in clay; he notices his father leaning on the wall in conversation with the cattle–dealer Farrell. But then he hears the word "Moran" and he opens the door to hear his father's words: "It was my father's voice. He was excited".

He hears his excited father say to Farrell:

'I know. I heard the exact sum. They got ten thousand dollars when Luke was killed. Every American soldier's life is insured to the tune of ten thousand dollars….. I heard they got two hundred and fifty dollars a month each for Michael and Sam while they're serving."

The son says he 'closed the door [of the lavatory] and stood in the darkness, in the smell of shit and piss and the warm fleshy smell of worms crawling in too little clay'. The stench of urine, excrement and the worms which will devour his dead body, place the son firmly in the grave and are a grim foretaste of death. Looking back on the incident from the future, the son says 'The shock I felt was the shock I was to feel later when I made some social blunder, the splintering of self-esteem and the need to crawl into a lavatory to think'. This is a crucial epiphany in the story and marks the son's transition to adulthood and the certain awareness that we will all die.

There is a detailed description of Luke Moran's funeral: an elaborate affair with the American flag draped over the coffin and shots fired over the grave 'before they threw in the clay'. The description of Luke Moran's funeral is not to mourn Luke again, but to show the son's thinking and the conclusion he comes to. The son has been thinking and repeats the outlines of his father's plan: 'He'd scrape the fare, I'd be conscripted there, each month he'd get so many dollars while I served, and he'd get ten thousand if I was killed'.

And this is the turning point of the story. The son says 'In the darkness of the lavatory between the boxes of crawling worms before we set the night lines for the eels I knew my youth had ended'. The son began the story like the young man executed at Mountjoy, but his moment of epiphany in the lavatory has removed the blindfold from his eyes and he sees clearly the reality of death – the stink of the shit, piss and the crawling worms reinforcing his understanding. He will die one day – but not in Korea fighting for America. 'Korea' began with an account of two violent deaths; it ends with the emotionally violent death of the son's innocence and youth.

At the end of the story they take to the river again; this time the son is rowing and the father is baiting the hooks. The son expresses his admiration for his father: 'I rowed as he let out the night line, his fingers baiting each twisted hook so beautifully that it seemed a single movement'. The father returns to his role as questioner: "Have you thought about what I said about going to America?" The son answers that he has decided not to go. The father is quite critical:

"You won't be able to say I didn't give you the chance when you come to nothing in this fool of a country. It'll be your own funeral".

The father is unaware that his conversation with Garrett was overheard by his son, but as readers we appreciate the irony of the son's agreement: "It'll be my own funeral," echoing the father's words. And this from the son who has had a funeral for his innocence in the lavatory, and described the pomp and ceremony of Luke Moran's funeral.

The son asks the father: "As you grow older, do you find your own days in the war and jails coming much back to you?" The father's long answer to this question ties together key elements of the story:

"I do. And I don't want to talk about them. Talking about the execution disturbed me no end, those cursed buttons bursting into the air. And the most I think is that if I'd conducted my own wars, and let this fool of a country fend for itself, I'd be much better off today. I don't want to talk about it."

He ignores the fact that if he had not fought in the Irish War of Independence there would be no Ireland to fend for itself, and he seems oblivious to the hypocrisy of encouraging his son to go to fight in someone's else's war – America's war in Korea.

Father and son take to the river again to set the lines for that night's eel-capture. The have talked again about the Irish War of Independence, but they do not touch on the metaphorical war they have been having about going to America – indeed, they have not mentioned explicitly at all the son fighting in Korea. The son's youth and innocence have been metaphorically murdered in the lavatory as he overheard his father's words to Farrell. There is also a sense that the son is metaphorically murdering his father's livelihood, since the father's financial positon is poor and will get worse as the son leaves to follow a profession or go to university.

The story began with an account of an execution of two men. It ends with the narrator having his own innocence 'murdered'. But the narrator, far from being upset by overhearing his father's plans for him, feels closer than ever to his father:

As the boat moved through the calm water and his line slipped through his fingers over the side I'd never felt so close to him before, not even when he'd carried me on his shoulders above the laughing crowd to the final.

Why does he feel so close to him? Because now father and son share the maturity and wisdom of adulthood: the son started the story like the blind-folded young man about to be executed; he ends the story eyes wide open like the older man.

The last sentence of the story is vital to its meaning: 'Each move he made I watched as closely as if I too had to prepare myself for murder'. The son now understands that adult life can be a series of metaphorical murders – the end of a relationship, a change in a relationship, a disagreement, an argument – and he now shares that knowledge of maturity with his father.

Irish Economic Stagnation

In describing America as the "land of opportunity" to his son the father is resorting to cliché, although Luke Moran's family have been well-rewarded for the death of their son. There are frequent references to the father's precarious economic situation and to the fact that it will worsen when the son is no longer there to help him. The father makes frequent disparaging remarks about Ireland and the limited possibilities for men of ambition.

Irish Emigration

The section on context made clear that Ireland has suffered from emigration for well over a hundred years. The usual reason is to find a better life economically.

The Son's Epiphany – from Innocence to Experience

The moment in the lavatory when the son overhears his father talking about Luke Moran is an epiphany because the son, surrounded by the smells of decay – urine, excrement and the worms – comes to a full appreciation that he will die: not as an American soldier in Korea, but one day.

It surprises some readers that the son does not react with anger at his father's 'plan' for him. However, there are circumstances which mitigate the father's enthusiastic talk of Luke Moran. Firstly, the father mentions America to the son – but he never mentions the Korean War and the financial benefits that would accrue to him: indeed, he puts his son under no real pressure to go. Secondly, the son does feel some guilt: he knows that his leaving will worsen his father's financial position.

Most importantly, as the last sentence of the story reveals, life involves a series of murders – mainly metaphorical – which sometimes have to be carried out. At the end of the story father and son are united in the knowing, shared maturity of adulthood – eyes wide open.

'A Family Supper' – Kazuo Ishiguro

Author

Kazuo Ishiguro was born in Nagasaki, Japan, on 8 November 1954. He came to Britain in 1960 when his father began research at the National Institute of Oceanography, and was educated at a grammar school for boys in Surrey.

Afterwards he worked as a grouse-beater for the Queen Mother at Balmoral before enrolling at the University of Kent, Canterbury, where he read English and Philosophy. He was also employed as a community worker in Glasgow (1976), and after graduating worked as a residential social worker in London. He studied Creative Writing at the University of East Anglia, a member of the postgraduate course run by Malcolm Bradbury, where he met Angela Carter, who became an early mentor. He has been writing full-time since 1982. In 1983, shortly after the publication of his first novel, Kazuo Ishiguro was nominated by *Granta* magazine as one of the 20 'Best of Young British Writers'. He was also included in the same promotion when it was repeated in 1993.

He has gone on to achieve great success and critical acclaim for a series of novels: *A Pale View of Hills* (1982), *An Artist of the Floating World* (1986), *The Remains of the Day* (1989), *The Unconsoled* (1995), *When We Were Orphans* (2000), *Never Let Me Go* (2005) and *The Buried Giant* (2015). If you want to read more Ishiguro, I would recommend *Never Let Me Go* as most suitable for your age group. This short story was first published in the journal *Firebird 2* edited by T J Binding and is also collected in *The Penguin Book of Modern British Short Stories* edited by Ray Bradbury.

Context

After the Second World War, at the end of which Japan had to surrender unconditionally, the country was devastated. All its major cities lay in ruins and two of its largest cities – Hiroshima and Nagasaki – had been completely destroyed and lay in ruins. It was also occupied by American troops. But the physical damage to the country of Japan was just as bad as the national humiliation and trauma that followed such an overwhelming defeat. Perhaps this explains why eating fugu became extremely popular in Japan after the war.... It was all the rage to perform the hazardous gutting operation in one's own kitchen, then to invite neighbours and friends round for the feast. Given the circumstances after the war, it must have seemed a brave but foolhardy thing to do – to eat fugu, given the possible poisonous effects. The fact that it became popular and people were prepared to accept the consequences (death by poisoning) demonstrates how demoralized Japanese citizens had become after their defeat in the Second World War. As we will see later, suicide plays an important role in the story and in traditional Japanese society.

Despite all the destruction it caused, the USA gave Japan massive assistance to rebuild its cities and develop its economy – partly to avoid a militaristic Japan causing another war. There was a general Americanisation of Japanese business and economic life. This is reflected in the story because the son has spent a few years in California and the daughter is planning to go hitch-hiking in California. The negative effects are seen when the father complains that 'Business these days has become so different. Dealing with foreigners. Doing things their way'. We find out as the story progresses that the father has retired early after the failure of his business and that he served in the Japanese navy during the Second World War.

Japanese Words

fugu – the Japanese name for puffer fish. As the narrator explains, if the fish is not prepared properly it is extremely poisonous and always proves fatal.

Kamakura district – the first and most powerful shogunate, established in the 12th century. Ishiguro's choice of it as the location for his story emphasises the past of Japan and is appropriate for the father who was 'particularly proud of the pure samurai blood that ran in his veins'. Samurai were traditional Japanese fighting men who would have protected the shogunate – which itself was a centre of power, learning and government and administrative control, the beginning of a central government in Japan.

tatami – a type of mat traditionally used as flooring in Japanese houses.

kimono – a traditional Japanese woman's dress.

Plot

The story is narrated by a young Japanese man who has arrived home in Japan after living in California for two years. We are not told why he left Japan or what he was doing in California; the narrator only says 'My relationship with my parents had become strained around that period'. Ishiguro's narrator tells us little if anything of what he is feeling and the story also proceeds by conversation (rather reserved and stilted) between the three characters - The topic is referred to again but the actual reason for the strain in his relationship with his parents is never specifically mentioned. The father has picked up his son from the airport, but their conversation is strained although the father tells his son that his business partner, Watanabe, committed suicide after their firm went bankrupt.

Shortly after they arrive at the family house, the narrator's younger sister. Kikuko, arrives, excited to see her brother again but answering her father with 'short formal replies'. The narrator and his sister both relax when the father leaves the room to prepare supper and they decide to go for a walk in the garden. Brother and sister converse more freely in the garden. Kikuko reveals that Watanabe did not only kill himself – he killed his wife and his two daughters as well.

Brother and sister stop at a well. As children the brother had told his sister that the well in the garden was haunted and as a child Kikuko 'never came out here alone'. In the story she peers down the well and claims "I can't see any ghosts". However, her brother claims to see one at that very moment standing in "a small clearing some ten yards away". He claims to have seen:

"An old woman. She was just standing there, watching me.... She was wearing a white kimono.... Some of her hair had come undone. It was blowing around a little."

This ghost will have further significance later in the story and will be discussed in the commentary.

Brother and sister re-enter the house to see how supper is progressing. The father orders Kikuko to oversee the meal, while he and his son take a tour of the house. The son has forgotten how large the house is, but notes that his father uses very few of the rooms. Finally they come to a room 'packed full of books and papers'. The father has even made a plastic model of a Japanese battleship, explaining to his son that he has a lot of time on his hands now he is retired. The father reveals that he believes that "your mother's death was no accident", implying that she accepted her friend's dinner invitation knowing there was a chance of being poisoned by fugu fish. The father adds that his wife had "many worries. And some disappointments". The son replies "Surely... my mother did not expect me to live here forever?" – which suggests that the family disagreed with the son's decision to move out of the house and live in California.

The father reveals that he served in the Japanese Navy during the war, but wishes he had served in the Air Force:

"If your ship was struck by the enemy, all you could do was struggle in the water hoping for a lifeline. But – in an aeroplane – well – there was always the final weapon."

Here the 'final weapon' was the aircraft itself which Japanese pilots – the kamikaze pilots – would deliberately crash into American ships in order to damage or destroy them.

They return to the dining room for supper. The narrator notices a photograph of an old woman in a white kimono – a woman he does not recognize. His father is angry that the son does not recognize his own mother and the son takes a closer look at the photo in the frame. He comments "She looks a lot older" and excuses his lack of recognition on the general darkness of the room beyond the dining area.

At the end of the meal the father asks Kikuko to make tea and he and his son talk. Specifically they talk about Watanabe's decision to kill himself and his whole family too. The father replies:

"Watanabe was very devoted to his work.... The collapse of the firm was a great blow to him. I fear it must have weakened his judgement."

The son presses him still further until the father admits that he sees Watanabe's actions were a "mistake" and that "There are other things besides work".

The father says his son is welcome to move back home, but the son's replies are non-committal. The father ends the story by expressing the expectation that Kikuko will move back home after she finishes her studies – but as readers we know (and the narrator knows) that is not going to happen, as Kikuko has plans to travel to California after she has finished her studies. The narrator knows this but answers his father evasively "Perhaps she will [come home]". The father is confident that "Things will improve then", to which the son replies "Yes, I'm sure they will".

The story ends with a single sentence which feels like an anti-climax because nothing in the story and nothing in the life of the family has been resolved: 'We fell silent once more, waiting for Kikuko to bring the tea'.

Characters

The Mother

The mother of the family is dead and has died after eating fugu, prepared by a friend two years before the events of the story. The mother did not usually eat fugu but 'was anxious not to offend' the 'old schoolfriend' who had invited her to dinner' – an indication of the traditional mores of Japanese society – the desire not to offend. Later in the story the father admits to the son that "It's my belief your mother's death was no accident", implying that she ate the fugu knowing there was a high chance she would die.

The Father

The son gives us a vivid sense of what his father looks like and his personality:

My father was a formidable-looking man with a large stony jaw and furious black eyebrows…. His general presence was not one which encouraged relaxed conversation, neither were things helped much by his odd way of stating each remark as it were the concluding one. In fact… a boyhood memory came back to me of the time he had struck me several times across the head for 'chattering like an old woman'. Inevitably, our conversation since my arrival at the airport had been punctuated by long pauses.

So the father is quite an authoritarian figure to his children: Kikuko smokes and has a boyfriend, and she lets her brother know these things, but she keeps these things secret from her father – frightened and intimidated by his probable negative reaction and disapproval. Later when the father leaves to prepare supper, the narrator tells us 'My sister relaxed quite visibly when he had left the room'. Part of the father's problems now are loneliness. He takes his son on a tour of the house, but 'the rooms were startlingly empty. The father comments, "This house is too large for a man to live in alone. I don't have much use for most of these rooms now." It is easy to see why he encourages the son and the daughter to move back into the family house. However, the father and son eventually reach a room that the father does use – full of books and papers, with flowers in vases and paintings on the wall. The father has been making a plastic model of a battleship very like the one he served on during the war, as he says, now he no longer has a business to run, "Since the firm folded… I have a little more time on my hands." This is litotes (deliberate understatement)– in fact, he has far too much time on his hands.

The father frequently says that Kikuko is "a good girl", but he does not know of her smoking or that she has a boyfriend – nor that she is thinking of going hitch-hiking in California. He frequently fails to treat her as an independent adult: when the son and daughter re-enter the house, the father asks Kikuko to finish preparing the meal by cooking the vegetable and keeping an eye on the other pots; after the meal he asks her to make some tea. On both occasions she pauses and looks at him before doing what he asks. In a family that is so bad at communicating with each other, the pauses are significant – she resents being used as a domestic dogsbody.

Quite apart from the Japanese context of the story and the aftermath of the war, the father does not live a happy life: he is old; he is a widower; he lives alone in a house which is far too big for one person; his business has folded and he has lots of time on his hands; and he has to cook and fend for himself. When Kikuko comments that 'Father's become quite a chef since he's had to manage on his own' he looks at her coldly and replies "Hardly a skill I'm proud of". He is not proud of it because he has grown up in a society where it is the wife's job in the family to cook. He is old, lonely and isolated – hence his hope that both his son and daughter will move back home to live in the house. But his final comment that "things will improve" when Kikuko comes back home to live is bleakly ironic, since the reader knows that Kikuko intends to go travelling in America or stay in Osaka. Furthermore, despite his invitation to his son to stay at home, the reader senses that this will not happen.

The son

Despite narrating the story in the first person, the son never gives the reader any insight into his feelings or thoughts, nor any internal reaction to anything that is said to him. In a way this is appropriate to the story since the characters in the story are reserved and reticent with each other – leaving much unsaid. Throughout the story there are long silences, the father in particular having at times very little to say.

We do know that the son has been living in America for a couple of years and that 'my relations with my parents had become somewhat strained around that period' – although we are never told precisely why they had become strained. It seems his decision to live in America may have triggered this strained relationship: later the son tells the father "Surely… my mother did not expect me to live here forever." The father's reply is noteworthy: "You don't see how it is for some parents.

Not only must they lose their children, they must lose them to things they don't understand" which implies that the mother could not understand the younger generation's obsession with America.

It may strike us as unusual that the son did not return for his mother's funeral or even discover the circumstances of her death until he returns to Tokyo. We are never told the reason for the strain in his relationship with his parents – perhaps it was his decision to go and live in California? We do know that it upset his mother and father deeply: the father tells him: "I for one am prepared to forget the past. Your mother too was always ready to welcome you back – upset as she was by your behaviour."

On several occasions throughout the story the father expresses the hope that the son's visit will not be a short one and even that he will move back into the family house, but the son's replies are always non-committal: "I'm not sure what my plans are"; when asked if he will stay in Japan, he replies "To be honest, I hadn't thought that far ahead"; when told he is welcome to move back into the family home, he replies "I'll have to think about it." Everything is left vague and ambivalent.

Kikuko

The narrator says that he and his sister 'had always been close'. She seems intimidated by her father and the conversation when her father is around is stilted and unnatural: she gives 'short formal replies' to his questions about her studies at Osaka. But as soon as the father leaves the room to prepare supper 'My sister relaxed quite visibly once he had left the room'. As soon as she is alone with her brother in the garden, her replies are less formal and she starts to talk more openly. She also smokes a cigarette, indicating that her father does not know she smokes and taking care to conceal the discarded butt beneath some pine needles in the garden.

During the meal Kikuko does not speak at all: she puts the mother's photograph back on the wall when handed it by the father and 'obediently' goes to make a pot of tea at the end of the meal when politely asked to by the father. Kikuko is clearly intimidated by her father and sees him as a powerful authority figure. It is difficult to square the silent, subdued Kikuko when her father is present with the vivacious young woman she proves herself to be in conversation with her brother.

Watanabe

Watanabe was the father's business partner who committed suicide when the business went bankrupt because 'he didn't wish to live with the disgrace'. The father reveals his suicide on the drive back from the airport. Kikuko tells the son later in the garden that Watanabe also took his wife and two young daughters with him by turning on the gas. The father's attitude to Watanabe is ambivalent: on the one hand, he calls him "A man of principle and honour. I respected him very much." However, later in the story the son gets his father to admit that Watanabe's suicide and in particular his killing of his whole family was "a mistake". We think that the father understands what Watanabe did – he says "The collapse of the firm was a great blow to him. I fear it must have weakened his judgment." Earlier in the garden Kikuko shows the different attitude of the younger generation, expressing sympathy for his daughters "Those two beautiful little girls" and concludes that the action was "sick".

The Ghost in the Garden

This began as a childhood joke invented by the son to tease and frighten his younger sister. Now they can talk about it with affectionate nostalgia. Kikuko thought that the ghost of an older woman lived in the well. The son responds by saying that he saw the ghost just standing in the garden: "It was an old woman.... She was just standing there watching me.... She was wearing a white kimono.... Some of her hair had come undone". It is significant in the story because in the photo the son does not recognize his own mother, she too is wearing a while kimono and, the son remarks, "She looks a lot older" – apparently it was taken just before her death, which, the father had told the son "was no accident" – she knew the risks of eating fugu and willingly accepted death, according to the father, because "She had many worries, And some disappointments." I think it is possible to see the figure of the old woman and the narrator's mother as symbols of an old Japan and old Japanese customs and rituals, in which suicide was considered an honourable and noble death.

The Second World War

The Second World War is mentioned at the opening of the story when the son explains the rage for fugu parties in its immediate aftermath. The generation born after the war are less concerned with traditional Japanese customs and have broader horizons – the son's leaving to live in California and Kikuko's desire to go there perhaps. The aftermath of the war has brought changes to business too: the father laments 'Business these days has become so difficult. Dealing with foreigners. Doing things their way'. He tells his son "I am – in retirement. I'm too old to involve myself in new ventures now." The younger generation has avoided the humiliation of losing the war and are more receptive to Western values – as Kikuko shows by having a boyfriend and taking up smoking, both of which she keeps secret from the father since she knows he will disapprove.

Suicide

Towards the end of the Second World War, Japan was losing the war against American forces who were steadily advancing towards the Japanese home islands. To defend Japan, special units of the Japanese air force were formed, known as kamikaze pilots (the name literally means "Divine Wind"); their official name was Special Attack Unit. Japan had lost its naval superiority by late 1944 and the kamikaze pilot's job was to destroy American ships by deliberately crashing their planes into American warships and in doing so, losing their own lives. Kamikaze pilots were on suicide missions, prepared to sacrifice their lives for the defence of Japan. Their sacrifice was seen both as a religious and a patriotic obligation. The planes the kamikaze pilots flew were specially adapted and packed with explosive materials in order to maximize damage to the American ships. Kamikaze pilots who failed to complete their mission – for whatever reason – were ostracized after the war and held in contempt for their failure to kill themselves for the sake of Japan.

To understand why the failed pilots were ostracized it is important to understand Japanese attitudes to suicide. In Europe suicide has, for centuries, been condemned by the church as a sinful and selfish act. By contrast, suicide in Japan has a long and honourable tradition dating back many centuries. In Japan suicide has been seen as an acceptable response to failure or defeat in battle. At the end of the Second World War many leading Japanese officers committed suicide to avoid the shame of unconditional surrender. In Japanese society an individual's identity is not valued as much as acceptance by society and conformity to society's mores. Therefore, how you are perceived by others is very important. If one feels ostracized or alienated from one's society, then suicide is still seen in Japanese culture as an acceptable response.

In 'A Family Supper' there are numerous references to suicide. Watanabe killed himself and his wife and two young daughters because he was so ashamed at the collapse of the business he ran with the father. There is a suggestion that the mother's death was no accident and that she willingly ate fugu knowing there was a possibility she might die. The father, who was in the Japanese Navy during the war, expresses half-serious regret that he was not in the air force and missed out on being a kamikaze pilot. Some readers have even suggested that the fish the father serves for supper is fugu – and that he plans for himself and his son and daughter to die. We deal with this controversial issue later.

Family Breakdown

Despite the title of this section, it is not true to say that the relationships in this family have broken down: they eat a meal together; they act with politeness to each other; the father and son even laugh together.

No, the real problem the family has is the inability to communicate freely, openly and without inhibitions. It is easy to blame the father since he is not very talkative, nor is he very curious about his son's stay in America. The son and the daughter are culpable too: when asked to make the pot of tea after the meal Kikuko stares at her father silently and pauses before going to do it – she could have made a verbal response. At the end of the story too, when the father is talking to the son about Kikuko's return to the house, the son could have tactfully suggested that this was unlikely to happen. All members of the family are complicit in the shadowy world of what is left unsaid.

The Loneliness of Old Age

This point has been made before, but it is worth repeating. If the story is partly about the torn loyalties that divide the generations in post-war Japan, this is also a story that highlights the plight of the old. The father, according to the son, was "always so busy". The father replies by saying that "Since the firm folded… I have a little more time on my hands." He laughed again, rather strangely. For a moment his face looked almost gentle. "A little more time." When the father says he should have been less busy and a more attentive father, the son laughs.

In truth, the father has nothing to do after a lifetime devoted to work. His wife is dead; his house is so big that he uses only a very small part of it; and he lives alone – no wonder he is so keen for one or both of his children to come home and live in the family house.

Reticence

'Reticence' means restrained or reserved and inclined to keep one's thoughts and feelings to oneself. In 'A Family Supper' there are many secrets or rather things that, as readers, we are not told and, to mirror this narrative reticence, there are many things that the characters do not tell each other. Likewise the narrator shares none of his thoughts and feelings with us. This has profound implications for the end of the story. The father seems to expect his son to return to America, but thinks that Kikuko will return to the family house to live… which the reader knows she will not do.

Therefore, the final exchange between father and son contains a bleak irony:

"Kikuko is due to complete her studies next spring," he said. "Perhaps she will want to come back home then. She's a good girl."

"Perhaps she will."

"Things will improve then."

"Yes, I'm sure they will."

The irony is that under no circumstances will Kikuko return home – and the son knows this too, so he is entirely complicit in the lack of communication that is going on here. The characters speak to each other but no communication takes place. The story ends on a note of calm but it is a false calm since it is based on an assumption that is false – Kikuko will not return home.

The Ending

Some readers have suggested that the fish the father serves for supper is fugu and he is planning to kill himself and his son and daughter. However, the textual evidence does not support this conclusion. Although the father praised Watanabe as a man of integrity and honour, he also agrees with his son that what Watanabe did was a mistake. He says "The collapse of the firm was a great blow to him. I fear it must have weakened his judgement." He goes on to say "There are other things beside work".

He also talks with optimism about Kikuko's eventual success in her studies and the possibility that she may return home to live – although the reader knows she won't. The father is destined to grow old alone in his large house making models of battleships to fill in the time.

'Invisible Mass of the Back Row' – Claudette Williams

Author

Claudette Williams spent the first years of her life in Heartease, Jamaica. Her father migrated to England in 1957 and her mother followed to join him in 1960. Claudette and her brother stayed in Jamaica and lived with her Aunt Salna, until they were able to join their parents in England in 1965. Claudette Williams learned about Black history from reading books, not from school history lessons. When she arrived in England she was unsure what to call her mother and she felt cold all the time. At her secondary school in England she was put in Band 5 (the second lowest band). The story is widely seen as autobiographical with Hortense representing Claudette Williams herself.

Context

The story is set in both Jamaica and England. Hortense, the narrator, is a black schoolgirl who lives with her stern aunt – her parents live in England. The story describes how Hortense responds, when instructed to recite the lesson of the day – she is expected to recall facts and figures about Christopher Columbus but, despite her nervousness, her response is impudent. Her parents eventually send for her, after some seven years, and she is transported to a strange new land, England. She remains seated at the back of the class, in the second from lowest set: 'I simply settle down to school life and cultivate the culture of the back row'. However, Columbus comes back to haunt her: this time she is prepared – having left her homeland she has explored her cultural heritage and is able to answer the teacher with a new found clarity. Putting aside the formulaic dates and times requested of her, she responds with the true facts of the conquest, much to the chagrin of the teacher.

We are not told what the date is in this story. However, there are a few clues: As mentioned previously, this story is both fictional and autobiographical and so we can assume that it is 1965, the year in which the author herself moved to the UK. There are references to cars, aeroplanes, Woolworths (the high street retailer, now disbanded) and paraffin heaters, in addition Hortense receives an education in Jamaica* – if we take a median of these details this dates the story to around 1965, as above.

'Invisible Mass of the Back Row' explores the transition of a girl from one culture to another and how, when removed from that culture, she begins to nurture a pride in her history and heritage. The story is, as much as anything, a celebration. It also looks at educational discrimination, colourism and the inadequacies of how history has recorded both the slave trade and the conquest. The following is extracted from an autobiographical essay by the author, in which she examines racism in the 1960's Jamaican educational system:

My school experience reinforced colourism. It taught me that it was the fair skinned children who received praise and the teacher's attention, and the Black children who were relegated to the back of the classroom.

*During the 1960's Jamaica's educational system underwent many changes: previously education had been scarce and was limited to shaping future workers under colonial rule. The onus of lessons had been focussed on domestic skills - the skills of servitude and the three 'R's': reading, writing and arithmetic. As self-rule gained momentum and as complex forces ignited after World War II, education became available to all and the scope of what was taught broadened to include additional subjects such as History and Geography.

Plot

In the first part of the story the narrator, Hortense, recalls a lesson in which the school inspector was present. She is challenged to recite dates and names in conjunction with Columbus' arrival on the island. Despite her nervousness: 'The stench of fear is in everyone's nostrils...', she answers with impudence: "'What was Columbus doing here anyway?' The trapped words in my head tumble out....' This incites her teacher, Miss Henderson, to crack a ruler over her hand. From Hortense's perspective her teacher is equally nervous in the presence of the inspector. The narrator reveals herself to be somewhat a rebel in these opening paragraphs. Although she is scared herself, she cannot seem to help herself: 'My brains, what brains I have left, are bouncing around in my skull, goading me on'. She also reveals that her aunt, whom she lives with, is equally terrifying: 'If Miss Henderson does not kill me with this ruler, my aunt is sure to finish me off when she hears how I back-chat the Inspector and Teacher Henderson'.

The narrator then informs the reader that her parents are in England and she describes living with her aunt as 'walking a tight-rope'. Hortense is then given a reprieve for her insolence in the form of the lunch bell. Her choice of words when describing the bell's consequence is akin to the language of emancipation, suggesting a growing interest in her cultural legacy: 'From outside there is the **freedom** of **released** bodies bouncing against the partition and **liberated** voices rising. They magnify our **imprisonment**. But the walls have been **breached**. The **jailors** are quick to realise that this **battle** is lost. For now'.

In the next section Hortense reveals a bullying side to her nature: she feels someone must pay for the incident, despite having incited the teacher and inspector herself. She picks on Lorna Phillips: "yo red pickney (paler skinned child) always sit at de front of de class. Unno t'ink is because yu pretty. Is only 'cause teacher frighten fi yu pupa." Lorna replies: "Is 'cause yu black and stupid why teacher meek yu sit a de back all de time." Hortense then calls on her peers to pursue Lorna with a view to beating her up (she is lighter skinned, rich and teacher's pet, which riles the narrator: 'She will pay for being teacher's favourite...for having everything I don't have').

Teacher Edwards appears on the scene and the pursuit is dropped. The narrator describes him as 'handsomely dressed in his Dashiki suit', she also reveals that 'there is a kindness about this man...we respected and even liked him'. When the 'running stops, slows to a polite walk' 'the hot pursuit melts into fixed grins and prim steps'. Lorna uses this as a means of escape.

Hortense excuses her actions by blaming them on the incident with the inspector: 'It is the pain of the inspector that has fuelled my blood; the pain of the ruler was nothing. Chu, mi use to beatings'. And so we are led to understand that the protagonist is used to physical punishment.

The narrator reveals not only a bigotry toward paler skinned black people but also rich black people, she bundles the inspector (who is black) into the same category as Lorna Phillips: 'Dis warra warra man, jus' a brother people head. Him 'now de score. After all him is suppose to be black...Lorna Phillips and de Inspector dem all de same. Have plenty of money and hate we'.

The next segment of the story describes how the children take their lunch. They are served by women of the village who bring a vast array of food. Lunch appears to be a social occasion and provides respite from the strictures of school: 'We mingle, swap and taste each other's purchases, eat, talk with mouths full...'

Back at home the protagonist later muses on her position within class: 'Will I one day move from the back row? Would I be let off reciting the day's lesson, because I know it, just once...?'. Her musings are interrupted as a letter and big parcel arrive. She and her brothers have been summoned by their parents to England. At first Hortense is excited: 'Columbus can get lost. No more standing up in the middle of the class. No more hot, sweaty classroom. No more Teacher

Henderson. No more Inspector. Me a go a Englan'.

In the early morning the narrator prepares for her journey ahead. She dresses in the clothes sent by her parents and her hair has been freshly styled. Neighbours arrive to say their farewells and finally Hortense begins her journey to the airport. It is only then that she stops to consider the fact that she is leaving behind the only life which she has known. Her thoughts turn to a deceased Cousy, presumably an elderly female relative and she worries about who will tend her grave: 'Who will make sure that the weeds do not choke her roses?' Finally, they arrive at the airport and are transported to England.

The narrator describes the reunion of herself with her parents and how the passage of time has made them unfamiliar to her. She describes the departure from Jamaica as 'the beginning of my exile from Heartease', which emphasises what a seminal journey it was. Reflecting, the author has Hortense recite a poem contrasting England with Jamaica and indicating a yearning on the part of the protagonist to return there:

Parffin heaters
smell
always just coming
into cold dark places
afraid and
excited at the same
time
cold
smell
wanting to be elsewhere
in fact Jamaica

We then learn how the narrator addresses her mother with her aunt's name, Selna, for want of a different word: 'I fell back on old responses, familiar language'. She reveals that she 'dreaded answering (to) my mother's call'. Expanding on this she divulges: 'What do you answer when strangers call to you, but they are not strangers really, they are your mother and father?' Her mother tactfully takes her aside and says to her: "You had better decide what you are going to call me. You can choose from Mother, Mummy, Mum. The same goes for your father. You've got Dad, Daddy or Father to choose from." This assuages the narrator's nervous tension but she observes: 'No one told me I would need a new language in dis England'.

The next section describes the protagonist's interview at her new school. She sarcastically and somewhat self-deprecatingly describes how she is streamed: 'My impressive reading enrolled me in one five, the hottest, baddest stream in the first year, only second to one six, the remedial stream'. Hortense finds herself in familiar territory, describing her new group of peers as 'home from home'. It transpires that One Five is composed almost entirely of poor Jamaican girls, all new to England.

Herself, a girl called Joycelin and a Fay Green begin a discussion about slavery, instigated by the book Joycelin is reading. Columbus is mentioned once again about which the narrator says: 'This Man, Columbus keeps coming back to haunt me'. As the girls discuss the exploits of slavers, life on plantations and the fight slaves and the indigenous Indians waged for their freedom, the girls '...move back and forth between anger, total disbelief and downright outrage'. The information which they had not questioned when within their own culture is now readily accessible to them in this Western world and the girls undertake to educate themselves on their heritage. The conversation moves to freedom fighters, who 'the books tell them' are 'from our own back yard': Toussaint L'Ouverture, Sojourner Truth, Nanny, Cudjoe and Paul Bogle.

The girls' exploration into their history arms them with the tools to respond to their teacher with the truth of Columbus' legacy for

Jamaica. When Hortense is asked "Why did Columbus sail to the Indies in 1493, Hortense?" she responds with authority and pride 'indignantly, the back row comes into its own':

Columbus was looking for a new route to India, so that when he landed in the Caribbean he was good and lost; he thought he was in India. The people who befriended him were massacred and the rest enslaved to mine gold and cultivate sugar. When they died from diseases Europeans brought to the islands, they were replaced by Africans stolen from the Gold Coast of Africa, Miss.

The teacher is clearly mortified and shamed by the protagonist's stance and knowledge; the children watch 'a stream of red blood rush from the neck to the top of head'. Fay Green, emboldened by Hortense's response adds: "Hawkins traded trinkets for black African people, who were enslaved and shipped to the Carribean to slave on sugar plantations, to make sugar for English people's tea, Miss."

The story concludes with a distinct air of victory: '...class five, unusually dignified, stands up and leaves the room. Miss remains fixed to her chair'.; 'Voices are raised, claiming, proclaiming, learning the new language in dis here England'. The protagonist has answered the question she put to herself previously: 'Would I be let off from reciting the day's lesson, because I know it, just once?'

Jamaican Words and Patois/Patwah

Much of the dialect in this story is written in Jamaican Patois (or Patwah) and some of the things mentioned will perhaps not be familiar to you. Jamaican Patois first evolved in the 17th century, an upshot of slaves from West and Central Africa learning to speak the vernacular and dialectical forms of English – spoken by Western or European 'masters'. Jamaican Patois can be categorised as a Creole, a language based on other mother languages (English). Creole dialects are usually directly connected to a large movement of immigration of one culture to another. In essence, Patois' roots are directly attributable to the slave trade. To understand the story the following will help (if you read the sentences aloud, this can also help you to understand):

Chu – True

Facety/Facetiness – Feisty/Festiness

Pan – On

Pickney – Child

Red Pickney – Lighter skinned child

Background

It is important to know a little of the background of Jamaica in conjunction with Christopher Columbus to truly appreciate the story.

Columbus was an Italian explorer and navigator, who, under the auspices of the Catholic Monarchs of Spain, undertook four voyages across the Atlantic Ocean. His remit was to establish trade routes and colonies, tools with which to retain an edge with emerging western imperialism and economic competition, a means of entering the spice trade. In 1494 Columbus arrived in Jamaica and proceeded to annex the island for the benefit of the King and Queen of Spain. The indigenous people, the Tainos, were a gentle race but had heard of the brutality of Columbus' men and a futile skirmish ensued – won, of course, by the Spanish with their superior weaponry. During his fourth and final voyage Columbus became shipwrecked on the rocks of St Anne's Bay in Jamaica and it was a year before a rescue ship could be summoned.

Whilst stranded Columbus befriended the native people who supplied him and his men with provisions; however, his cohorts treated the indigenous people badly, stealing from them and, unsurprisingly, their source of food dried up. On board the ship Columbus had an almanac of astronomical tables and he discovered that a lunar eclipse was due. He used this to his advantage telling the people that his God was angry with them for their treatment of him and his crew. He informed the people that his God would provide a clear sign of his fury, in the form of a lunar eclipse. In essence, he scammed the local people through fear into continuing to supply him and his men with provisions.

Columbus' actions eventually paved the way for the Spanish settlement of Jamaica in 1510, headed up by Governor Juan de Esquivel. His cruelty and that of the Spanish colonists remains legendary. The indigenous Tainos became victims of European diseases and suffered terribly under the *ecomienda* system (hard labour with extreme punishment and death if resisted). This resulted in the wholesale obliteration of the Tainos and the practice of importing slaves from Africa.

Historical References

Again, to understand the story properly you need to have some background on the historical references within the story. Although these figures are referred to only briefly they are essential to the prevailing themes of the story – in particular racial discrimination, oppression and cultural heritage:

Toussaint L'Ouverture

Toussaint L'Ouverture was a self-educated slave. He had no military training but succeeded in driving Napoleon out of Haiti, leaving a legacy of independence and freedom from the slave trade. However, this was not before his betrayal at the hands of the French (on Napoleon's orders). Napoleon ordered his men to detain Toussaint in a prison where he would die of cold, starvation and neglect. After Toussaint died, his followers carried on the fight for freedom. Napoleon, when questioned about his appalling treatment of Toussaint, is alleged to have replied: "What could the death of one wretched Negro mean to me?"

Sojourner Truth

Sojourner Truth was born into slavery but escaped with her child in 1826. She was an African-American abolitionist and women's rights activist who sponsored broad and varied reform causes. Abolition was one of the few causes that Truth was able to see realized in her lifetime.

Paul Bogle

While slavery in Jamaica was purported to have been abolished in 1833 many former slaves remained in roles of servitude to their former owners; they were also subject to a judicial system controlled by the colonial government for the benefit of former slaveholders. Unemployment, high taxes and low wages were endemic within that regime. It was Paul Bogle who headed up a large-scale armed rebellion (the Morant Bay rebellion) for voting rights, an end to legal discrimination and economic oppression. Owing to his valour he was posthumously recognised as a national hero in Jamaica in 1969.

(Captain) Cudjoe

In the 'New World' (a term coined by the Florentine explorer, Amerigo Vespucci, to reflect the Western world's discovery of the Americas), black slaves had successfully escaped the oppression of their Spanish and Portugese captors, eking out a living in inland Jamaica, they were called 'Maroons' (from the Spanish word: 'cimarron' – feral, animal, fugitive, runaway). Cudjoe was a Maroon leader. In 1655 the English, commanded by Cromwell, successfully conquered Jamaica. They attempted, by military force and bribery, to drive the Maroons from the inlands and mountains, unsuccessfully. Even after offers of peace and liberty the Maroons declined. Peace was finally settled in 1739, under Cudjoe's leadership, and the Maroons were given self-governance in exchange for support against foreign invasion.

Nanny (Queen Nanny or Nanny of the Maroons)

Nanny was thought to have been born in what is now called Ghana, Western Africa, into the Ashanti tribe. History indicates that she was brought to Jamaica as a slave (with her brothers, one of whom was Cudjoe). Escaping from the plantations the family split up to establish Maroon colonies in inland Jamaica and by 1720 Nanny and her husband had settled and controlled an area in the Blue Mountains which was named Nanny Town. For over 30 years she is said to have been instrumental, through her skills in guerrilla warfare, for the release of scores of slaves. She remains a powerful symbol of the Maroons' resistance to slavery.

Characters

Hortense

Hortense is a poor, teenage, black, Jamaican girl and quite a complex character. She lives with her aunt and brothers in a 'tiny, two-roomed house' – her parents moved to the UK some time ago (her mother five years' ago and her father seven years' ago).

In the first part of the story Hortense reveals that she sits in the back row of class. It should be noted that, unlike in England, this is not a choice on the part of the pupil, the teacher makes this decision, apparently based upon skin tone and academic ability and Hortense describes her position as '…hidden, disposed of, dispatched to the invisibility of the back row'. The narrator also wonders whether she will ever be seated at the front: 'Would it ever be my turn to sit at the front?....' Perhaps because of her status, a back row dweller and what this is associated with, she is presented as a nervous student ('I stand up, my limbs shaking uncontrollably, sweat dripping from my armpits, my eyes inflamed....'), she is self-deprecating and is aware of her academic deficiencies: 'My brains, what brains I have left....' She, as the title suggests, and as mentioned above, feels invisible: 'Something tells me that my days of being hidden, disposed of, dispatched to the invisibility of the back row, are numbered'. Conversely, she is also somewhat a bully with very definite opinions. After the incident with the inspector she channels her fury into a paler skinned Jamaican girl, despite her having nothing to do with Hortense's humiliation: 'But first there is Lorna Phillips to take care of. Somebody has to pay for this...' She addresses Lorna: "Yo red pickney always sit a de front of de class. Unno t'ink is because yu pretty. Is only 'cause teacher frighten fi yu pupa." Her bigotry is fuelled by her uncle ('My uncle say all a dem collude, not just me, but all a we, all de people who look like me. All de poor black people dem'.) and she therefore slots both the black inspector and the rich lighter-skinned girl into the same group: 'Meek him no pick pan de red pickney dem, a meek him t'ink say is we alone no know nothing'. ('Makes him not pick on the lighter skinned children, makes him think that we don't know anything').

Throughout the story Hortense is acutely aware, not only of her own skin tone: '...we have all recently arrived...from Jamaica and all poor, clearly black and one rung from the back row...', but of those of others. She describes Teacher Edwards as: '...beautifully dark...' and Miss Mavis as having: '...the most beautifully oiled, ivory coloured skin...' When Hortense is handed over to the air stewardess at the airport she describes her as: '...a pretty chocolate-coloured woman...' Her descriptions of the white people she encounters are far less flattering. She describes her teacher in Jamaica as having a: '...sharp pointed nose, mean eyes and frightened face'. Similarly, she describes her class mate, Lorna Phillips, as a 'red pickney'. In essence, although Hortense clearly feels victimised for her colour, she could also be seen to be exercising some racial stereotyping herself.

We know that the character has been subject to physical punishment, which was probably the norm in Jamaica in the 1960's: 'Chu, mi use to beatings. One little ruler slap a nothing....'

Despite the character's flaws she is also a caring child, she likes and respects the dinner ladies and she later reveals that she tends 'Cousy's' grave (presumed to be an elderly female relative). When she learns that she will be leaving Jamaica she asks: 'Who will look after Cousy's grave? Who will make sure that the weeds do not choke her roses?' When the family convene at the airport to wish Hortense and her brothers farewell the emotions described suggest that the narrator is part of a loving extended family: 'Now, everybody is crying, some pretending that they aren't....'

After the narrator arrives in the UK she finds certain things challenging: the language and dialect ('No one told me I would need a new language in dis England'.); the cold; missing home and residing with two relative strangers (her mother and father). However, at school she is quick to settle in:

In this group we have all recently arrived, from one island or another but mostly from Jamaica and all poor, clearly black and one rung from the back row...This is home from home. I simply settle down to school life and cultivate the culture of the back row. We graduate in hair plaiting, make up and cussing....

When Hortense and her new friends start to research their heritage, fuelled by their parting from Jamaica, she reveals herself to be a character of depth. On discovering the historical misinformation or omissions taught to them the girls: '...move back and forth between anger, total disbelief and downright outrage'. The character describes these conversations as: '...self-affirmation lessons which claim space in our section of the common-room'. At the end of the story Hortense, armed with fresh information concerning her birthright, speaks out with a confidence she did not have in Jamaica, telling the teacher the true impact Columbus had on her country.

The Inspector

We know little of the inspector, aside from the fact that he is black and relatively rich (from Hortense's perspective) and he is a source of fear to both the children and Miss Henderson. Williams introduces him to shine a spotlight on the oppressive style of teaching in 1960's Jamaica. The narrator's views on him are very clear and because we know that the story is part-autobiographical this lends an element of reliability to the narrative: 'Lorna Phillips and de inspector dem all the same. Have plenty of money and hate we'.

Miss Henderson

Miss Henderson, Hortense's teacher, is a fearsome character: '...with (her) sharp pointed nose, mean eyes and frightening face...' She is prepared to use physical punishment to redress Hortense's impudence: 'Before the last word has left my lips, the sharp sting of the ruler cracks my knuckles....' Again, Williams has introduced this character to highlight the austerity of teaching in Jamaica. We can assume she is white from her 'sharp pointed nose' so the author is also making reference to colourism – whereby those with lighter, fairer skin are treated with higher regard than those with dark skin. From the narrator's perspective, which reinforces this, Miss Henderson favours the lighter skinned girl, Lorna Phillips: 'Today she will pay for being teacher's favourite, for being "red", for being rich, for having everything I don't have'.

Lorna Phillips

Lorna Phillips takes the role of antagonist in this story, perhaps merely because of her lighter skin. The narrator abhors her for 'having everything I don't have'. She does not take Hortense's cruelty silently and is confident enough to counter with: "Is 'cause yu black and stupid why teacher meek yu sit a de back all de time..." From this we can conclude that Lorna considers herself superior owing to her colour – again, a reference to colourism. We can assume that her family, particularly her father, has a position of some authority and standing from Hortense's word: "Unno t'ink is because yu pretty. Is only 'cause teacher frighten fi yu pupa."

Teacher Edwards

Teacher Edwards appears just once in the story. He is described by the narrator as:

...big, sturdy and beautifully dark...handsomely dressed in his Dashiki suit. There is a kindness about this man that is not usually found among teachers. He would always listen to you, and not just take the teacher's side. He only beat you if he really feel you was out of order, or rude, or you get catch with something you thief. We respected and even liked him.

The description provided by Williams suggests that the narrator has a crush on this teacher; however, it is clear that despite being 'kind' he is also a man given to violence. This demonstrates how prevalent corporal punishment was in 1960s' Jamaica.

The lunch ladies

The narrator's description of the lunch ladies is generally favourable. Aunt Dine who 'smells of cinnamon': '...will give you a big smothering hug'. Miss Mavis: '...is never cross for long, but will cuss you out one minute and tell you scriptures the next. Her face is electric...Her eyes search your face for understanding' and Miss Ivy has a face that 'glows' They provide contrast in the story – many of the adults treat the children harshly in this story: lunch time provides a reprieve from the austerity of school.

Aunt Salna

We know that Aunt Salna is also given to violent reprimand. Hortense divulges that: 'My parents are in England and living with my aunt is like walking a tight-rope....' In addition she discloses that: 'If Miss Henderson does not kill me with this ruler, my aunt is sure to finish me off....' Aunt Salna is also clearly, and conversely, a caring relative who has taken the role of *loco parentis*, not just to Hortense but also her siblings, quite some undertaking over an extended period of time. When Hortense is preparing to leave Jamaica her aunt assumes responsibility for having her niece's hair styled and laying out her clothes for the voyage. She is a proud woman.

Cousy

Cousy is referred to just briefly. She is a deceased elderly relative of the protagonist, who clearly had a very strong bond with her. She is described in favourable terms and appears to have been a very caring woman to Hortense: 'Does this mean I won't ever share Cousy's bed and snuggle into her warm bosom? Won't smell her mysterious smells, and watch her crinkled face?'. When Cousy dies Hortense is moved to tears: "I want Cousy,' I hollered, as I fell into Miss Olive's arms'. Again, Cousy provides contrast in a story in which many of the adults have no qualms about corporal punishment.

Mother and Father

The parents in this story represent one of the first waves of immigration from Jamaica to the UK. During the 1950s a beleaguered UK looked to the colonies to fulfil labour shortages and actively encouraged migration from Jamaica. The vast majority of Jamaicans settled in London and were found work within the NHS and with London Transport and British Rail. It is likely, therefore, that Hortense's parents were motivated by pecuniary gain. When they first arrived they would not have had the means of supporting their existing family and would have had to make a very difficult decision in leaving them behind. We can assume that their summoning of their children from Jamaica meant that they had saved sufficiently to now support the family. The story tells us very little in terms of the father - his career and character are absent from the prose. However, the mother comes across as caring and patient. When Hortense addresses her with Aunt Salna's name she demonstrates a compassionate nature: 'Now listen to me child,' my mother's dark, youthful face smiles down at me... "You have better decide what you are going to call me. You can choose from Mother, Mummy, Mum. The same goes for your father...." This allays Hortense's dread: 'This little talk put an end to days of nervous tension about deciding what to call my England parents'."

Joycelin

Joycelin, Hortense's new friend in England, is also a black immigrant from Jamaica, together with Fay Green. She is the catalyst of the girls' re-education on Jamaican history and 'feeds' the trio information from books she takes out from the local library.

Fay Green

Hortense's other new friend in England is Fay Green. At first, Fay is incredulous with the information being disseminated to her: "Is who write dat book you reading? 'Cause is foolishness you telling me. I don't believe a word of it." Later, after Hortense voices her potted history of Jamaica in conjunction with Columbus, Fay becomes emboldened and contributes to the class: "Hawkins traded trinkets for black African people, who were enslaved and shipped to the Caribbean to slave on sugar plantations, to make sugar for English people's tea, Miss." The trio share not only hair oils and face powder but also 'self-affirmation lessons' and united, they undertake to deconstruct the limited history previously afforded to them. In so doing they bolster their sense of self-worth and when the class is dismissed: 'Whoops and slaps are heard down the corridor. The back row claims a victory. 'She won't be asking us those stupid questions again, will she?."

Miss (the teacher in England)

From the narrator's description, the English educational system – though different, is equally austere where: 'Group humiliation replaces individual humiliation...' She also provides: 'This bottom from remedial class gets the meanest, most feared teachers in the school. Their sole intention seem to be to ensure that we know and keep our place'. From deduction this suggests that 'Miss' is also a pretty mean character and when she poses the same formulaic questions as Hortense's teacher in Jamaica ("Why did Columbus sail to the Indies in 1493, Hortense?...", this provides the perfect opportunity for the protagonist to set the record straight:

Indignantly, the back row comes into its own. "Columbus was looking for a new route to India, so that when he landed in the Caribbean he was good and lost, he thought he was in India. The people who befriended him were massacred and the rest enslaved to mine gold and cultivate sugar. When they died from diseases Europeans brought to the islands, they were replaced by Africans stolen from the Gold Coast of Africa, Miss."

The teacher's obvious mortification in being out of her depth ('We watch the frozen face thaw out. We watch her eyes travel along the two rows at the back. We watch a stream of red blood rush from the neck to the top of her head') signals a victory for the children, not just over the teacher but for the truth of Jamaica's history.

Language

Jamaican Patois

Perhaps the most striking style element of the story is the use of Jamaican Patois - what Hortense speaks is often very different from the narrative. In speech the Patois can be difficult to understand at times: 'Meek him no pick pan de red pickney dem....', while her narrative is written in formal English with brief interjections of Patois: 'It is the pain of the inspector that has fuelled my blood, the pain of the ruler was nothing. Chu, mi use to beatings'. The author has probably mixed up the two dialects- the Patois and the formal English - to provide a better understanding on the part of the reader unfamiliar with the mother-tongue of Jamaica.

Narrative Viewpoint

The second most obvious device used in the story is the narrative viewpoint - the protagonist is also the exclusive author. Now living in England she recounts the story of her life in Jamaica, her departure and her new life in the UK. Because we believe that the story is, to a large degree, autobiographical this lends credence to the account.

Paragraph Structure

The story is broken up into small paragraphs and, when the author wishes to press home information, she uses one sentence paragraphs:

'I might not know the answers, but I can fight'.

'Lorna makes the most of Teacher Edwards' presence'.

"I want Cousy', I hollered, as I fell into Miss Olive's arms'.

'No one told me I would need a new language in dis England'.

'I was not to know then, that although I would return many times, that first departure was the beginning of my exile from Heartease'.

'Voices are raised, claiming, proclaiming, learning the new language in dis England'.

Similarly, Williams uses short sentences at the beginning of a paragraph to impress a point or set the scene: 'My heart pounds'. 'The boxes are unwrapped'; 'We go down the hill'; 'Boxes are empty'. These are followed by longer sentences which create a kind of rhythm to the story, more redolent of poetry and many of the paragraphs end with a short sentence to the same effect: 'We turn down the hill'; 'There is always tomorrow'; 'Have plenty of money and hate we'.

Metaphor

Williams carefully selects words associated with the slave trade to suggest a growing awareness in Hortense of her heritage:

From outside there is the ***freedom*** *of* ***released*** *bodies bouncing against the* ***partition*** *and* ***liberated*** *voices rising. They magnify our* ***imprisonment****. But the* ***walls*** *have been* ***breached****. The* ***jailers*** *are quick to realise that this* ***battle*** *is lost.*

The narrator's metaphor for school works extremely well and provides a clever device with which to steer the reader's thoughts toward slavery and emancipation.

Use of Adjectives and Repetition

The description of people and things is rich with adjectives, throughout the story, and this makes the people and things described come to life. Describing Mr Edwards, the narrator provides: 'His is big sturdy and beautifully dark, with a baby moustache'. And Miss Mavis is described as having: 'the most beautifully oiled, ivory coloured skin in the whole world, and white, white eyes which twinkle and wink at you when she talks....' In this latter description the author also uses repetition to emphasize detail, a device which appears several times during the story. 'Miss Henderson is afraid. She is as much afraid of the inspector as I am'; 'My brains, what brains I have left...'; 'The Headmistress was impressed. I was impressed. Mum was impressed. My impressive reading enrolled me in one five....' (p. 86) and 'English cold. English ice. Frozen faces, frozen information, frozen places'.

The Contrast of Heat

Williams often uses contrasting heat to create atmosphere: 'The hot pursuit melts...'; '...she got colder as the morning got warmer...'; 'I am cold in the blazing sunshine' and 'Easington heat. Easington sweat. English cold. English ice. Frozen faces, frozen information, frozen places....' The contrasting temperatures add real drama to the narrative.

Personification

The author draws on personification a number of times during the story. When the narrator recounts Cousy's death, she describes death as follows: 'Death had crept under the door and taken Cousy away in her sleep'. The use of the word 'creep' here, suggests that death had taken on the human trait of insidiousness or deception and creates a sinister atmosphere. Similarly as the family make their way to the airport the '...sun claims its place in the sky. It releases its passions...' and 'The Sun releases its enormous strength. The sea retaliates...' Williams attributes the elements with foreboding power just as Hortense is about to leave her country, this makes the protagonist appear diminutive and vulnerable by contrast. The author follows with the metaphor: '...we are sitting in the belly of the gigantic metal bird...' This serves to re-enforce Hortense's vulnerability, her life is at the mercy of this huge, unfamiliar object – something which perhaps she has never seen before; certainly, we can assume, that this is her first flight.

The Poem

Williams divides the story neatly into two with Hortense's poem. This is inserted after the line: 'I was not to know then, that although I would return many times, that first departure was the beginning of my exile from Heartease'. The poem describes her new climate with repetition of the word 'cold' twice - she confesses she misses Jamaica. After the poem the story is then set in England. The poem effectively demarcates the end of an era for the protagonist.

Themes

Colonialism & History

The story challenges not only colonialism but also how its history has been recorded. Columbus Day is still celebrated to this day and many states in America observe a day's holiday. However, traditional history and the teaching thereof, has often been constrained to dates and time and sanitised of any human suffering. When the New World was named, ironically and somewhat arrogantly, this took no account of the indigenous people who had already populated the countries 'founded'. 'Invisible Mass' challenges colonialism to its core. In both her Jamaican and English schools Hortense is expected to treat history dispassionately; the teachers wish to hear a regurgitation of sterile dates and times, taken from the Western world's perspective. However, when – together with her new friends in England – they embark on autonomous 'self-affirmation' lessons and explore the unsung histories of Toussaint L'Ouverture, Sojourner Truth, Nanny, Cudjoe and Paul Bogle, '...from our own back yard'. They begin to nurture a growing awareness of their true heritage and the 'rebels', 'heroes' and 'guerrilla fighters' who helped carve their freedom. They discover a pride in their background which culminates in Hortense finding the courage to set the record straight in the closing paragraphs of 'Invisible Mass'. She no longer feels invisible but jubilant and 'dignified'.

Educational Racism

The story also shines a spotlight on educational racism which was endemic in 1960's Jamaica. White Jamaicans took priority under colonial rule and it was many years before black Jamaicans were afforded an education. When that did happen the education was rudimentary and designed to mould future workers, preparing them for a life of servitude. School was a place to be feared and corporal punishment was the norm. The opening paragraphs demonstrate just how terrifying school would have been in 1960's Jamaica. The author describes the physical manifestation of Hortense's fear in paragraph 4: 'I stand up, my limbs shaking uncontrollably, sweat dripping from my armpits, my eyes inflamed....' School, to the protagonist is akin to the slavery of her forefathers and Williams uses words associated with the slave trade and emancipation to emphasize this: 'From outside there is the **freedom** of **released** bodies bouncing against the **partition** and **liberated** voices rising. They magnify our **imprisonment**. But the walls have been **breached**. The **jailors** are quick to realise that this **battle** is lost. For now'.

We know from the narrative that black girls from a poor background were made to sit at the back of the class, hence 'Invisible Mass of the Back Row'. From here the protagonist feels invisible, 'disposed of', whereas the paler girl, Lorna Phillips, always sits at the front as '...teacher's favourite, for being "red"'. And so, from this story, and history, we can conclude that even within the educational system there was a distinct hierarchy according to skin colour.

Colourism

Williams also explores the theme of Colourism, a term coined by the author Alice Walker in 1982. Whilst it may not have had a name in 1960's Jamaica it was certainly a very real entity. Colourism, more recently called 'pigmentocracy', is prejudice or discrimination against individuals with a dark skin-tone; those with fairer skin are treated more favourably and are treated as having a higher social status. In the modern world Colourism supports a multi-billion pound business in skin lighteners and is also often responsible for devastating effects, physically and psychologically.

The character, Hortense, is very aware of her own skin-tone and when she starts her education in England she is, once again, relegated to the back of the class. She observes: 'In this group we have all recently arrived, from one island or another but mostly from Jamaica and are all poor, clearly black and one rung from the back row....' The character Hortense is also keenly aware of the skin-tones of others. Teacher Edwards' skin is described as 'beautifully dark', Miss Mavis has 'the most beautifully oiled, ivory coloured skin....' and when Hortense and her brothers are handed over to the stewardess she is described as a 'pretty chocolate-coloured woman'. Hortense refers to lighter-coloured black people as being 'red': "Yo red pickney..." and when she picks on Lorna Phillips the author allows the paler coloured girl's retort to cement the notion of colourism: "Is 'cause yu black and stupid..."

In an autobiographical essay the author herself is said to have commented on 1960's Jamaica:

My school experience reinforced colourism. It taught me that it was the fair skinned children who received praise and the teacher's attention, and the Black children who were relegated to the back of the classroom.

'The Darkness Out There' – Penelope Lively

Author

Penelope Lively was born in Cairo, Egypt in 1933 and spent the first twelve years of her life there. Her family then moved to England at the end of World War Two. In England she boarded at a school in Sussex before attending St Anne's College, Oxford where she read Modern History.

Lively, a prolific writer with over 40 published novels, has been the recipient of a host of literary awards during her writing career. These include the Carnegie Medal for the children's book 'The Ghost of Thomas Kempe' (1973), the Whitbread Children's Book Award for 'A Stitch in Time' (1976), the Arts Council National Book Award for 'Treasures of Time' (1979) and the Booker Prize for Fiction for 'Moon Tiger' (1987).

Her short stories have appeared in The Literary Review, Good Housekeeping, Vogue, Cosmopolitan, The Observer and the New York Times. She was awarded the OBE in 1989, the CBE in 2002 and the DBE in 2012. In 1998 she was awarded an honorary doctorate from the University of Warwick.

Describing the purpose behind her writing she states: 'In writing fiction I am trying to impose order upon chaos, to give structure and meaning to what is apparently random. People have always sought explanations and palliatives for the arbitrary judgments of fate. I am an agnostic, and while I would not suggest the construction of fiction as an alternative to religious belief, it does seem to me that many writers – and I am certainly one – look at it as an opportunity to perceive and explain pattern and meaning in human existence'.

Lively's work is especially concerned with history and memory. She perceives memory, not in the context of a chronological time frame, but as an assortment of mental slides. 'The Darkness Out There' is a short story extracted from the collection *Pack of Cards,* published in 1984.

Plot

'The Darkness Out There' is written in the third person. It is set in the English countryside and in the home of an elderly widow. It begins with paragraphs of narrative, however, as the story progresses the narrative gives way to dialogue.

In the story school-girl Sandra (the protagonist) is a member of the Good Neighbours' Club. A club set up to help the elderly amongst the community. Miss Hammond, or Pat, who runs the Good Neighbour's Club assigns Sandra to help Mrs Rutter for the afternoon. As Sandra makes her way along a path to the elderly lady's cottage the narrative turns to Packer's End; a dense spinney at the edge of the path. Steeped in local folklore the woods hold a long-standing intrigue and association with menace. We learn that when Sandra was small the woods were thought to contain witches, wolves and tigers, later in childhood she became aware that a German aircraft had crashed in Packer's End. As a child you never went into Packer's End alone.

As Sandra progresses towards Mrs Rutter's home she bumps into Kerry Stevens, a boy from her school who has also been asked to help Mrs Rutter. When they have finished the various tasks Mrs Rutter has asked them to attend to they sit down to drink some tea. Mrs Rutter then recounts the story of the German aircraft.

The aircraft crashed into Packer's End on what Mrs Rutter describes as a 'filthy wet night, pouring cats and dogs'. She and her sister were alone in the house when it happened. They went to investigate and found that one of the crew was still alive but 'hurt pretty bad'. Mrs Rutter then tells the children how they left the airman unattended in the crashed plane for two nights. She gives a number of reasons for failing to notify the authorities: 'it was bucketing down, cats and dogs,' she discovered that her bike had a flat tyre and Dot her sister was 'running a bit of a temp'. She had, in fact, no intention of helping the airman for whom she displays utter contempt and mercilessness. In line 325 she tells the children:

I reckon he may have seen me, not that he was in a state to take much in. He called out something. I thought, oh no, you had this coming to you, mate, there's a war on. You won't know that expression – it was what everybody said in those days. I thought, why should I do anything for you? Nobody did anything for my Bill, did they? I was a widow at thirty-nine. I've been on my own ever since.

The children, appalled at her story and her treatment of the young airman, leave the house almost immediately. The story closes with Sandra's realisation that things are not always as they initially seem.

Setting and Time

The story is set in the countryside and in the home of Mrs Rutter, regional dialect is used but it does not establish exactly what part of the country the story refers to. Similarly, we know that the story was written in 1984, however, some of the references within the story suggest that time is a little more ambiguous. Sandra refers to Kerry as a 'stupid so-and-so' in line 82 and in line 251 when the German plane is brought into the conversation she confesses 'it always gives me the willies'. She dreams of a life rather more redolent of the 1950s, citing amongst her ambitions secretarial work. Both her language and expectations feel dated for 1984. Perhaps this is testimony to the author's age and the limited possibilities which would have been available to her as a young girl.

Characters

Sandra

Sandra is a girl with quite unremarkable and vague expectations of life. She tells Kerry in line 207 that she wants to be a secretary and in line

67 she relays her dreams: she would fall in love and she would get a good job and she would have one of those new Singers that do zig-zag stitch and make an embroidered coat'. We can assume that Sandra is at secondary school and on the cusp of puberty, the paragraph beginning at line 125 suggests a sexual awakening: 'The girl blushed. She looked at the floor, at her own feet, neat and slim and brown. She touched, secretly, the soft skin of her thigh; she felt her breasts poke up and out at the thin stuff of her top....' We know that Kerry is due to start work in July of the same year so, as his peer, we can deduce that Sandra is about fourteen or fifteen years' old.

She is quite a stereotyped version of a girl with her aversion to dirt and her perceptions of neatly classified male and female roles. Line 201: 'She thought of the oily workshop floors, of the fetid underside of cars. She couldn't stand the feel of dirt, if her hands were the least bit grubby she would go and wash'. And at line 208: 'Men didn't mind so much. At home, her dad did things like unblocking the sink and cleaning the stove....' Similarly, she happily accepts the tasks Mrs Rutter assigns to her, which are quite different to the typically male chores assigned to Kerry. Sandra identifies herself as a nervous character, line 176: 'She was nervy, she knew. Mum always said so'.

In the story Sandra's innocence gives way to a greater worldliness. She is used as a tool to demonstrate that things and people are not always as they seem. She demonstrates a shift from imagined child-hood fears to real horror at the atrocities of adulthood: 'You could get people wrong and there was a darkness that was not the darkness of tree shadows and murky undergrowth and you could not draw the curtains and keep it out because it was in your head, once known, in your head for ever like lines from a song....'

Kerry Stevens

We learn through Sandra that 'none of her lot reckoned much on (him)'. She describes him as having black-slicked down hair and slitty eyes. Volunteering her opinion of him she concludes that 'Some people you only have to look at to know they're not up to much'. However, Kerry is a young man who has volunteered his services to the elderly, so at once there is a tension between Sandra's analysis and the readers' own. On his physical appearance the narrator discloses that 'his chin was explosive with acne; at his middle his jeans yawned from his T-shirt showing pale chilly flesh'.

Kerry undertakes his assigned tasks without complaint and reveals to the old woman his equally modest ambitions to start working at the Blue Star garage with day release at 'the tech' after he has left school.

On learning of the airman's plight Kerry is the first to demonstrate outrage. While Sandra is clearly upset, Kerry's anger is palpable and manifests itself both verbally and physically: 'The boy said, "I'm not going near that old bitch again." He leaned against the gate clenching his fists on an iron rung; he shook slightly. "I won't ever forget him, that poor sod."

Pat/Miss Hammond

Pat plays a very minor role in this story, she is used as a device to set the initial scene. In the opening paragraph she describes Mrs Rutter in a way that suggests that she is both sweet and fragile: "Mrs Rutter at Nether Cottage, you don't know her, Sandra? She's a dear old thing, all on her own, of course, we try to keep an eye on her. A wonky leg after her op and the home help's off with a bad back (line 4)." As the story progresses this character analysis is challenged and finally reversed.

On Pat's physical demeanour, in the second paragraph we can assume that Sandra has adopted the role of narrator, she describes Pat: 'Pat had a funny eye, a squint, so that her glance swerved away from you as she talked. And a big chest jutting under washed-out jerseys (line 9)'. Sandra muses: "Are people who help other people always not very nice-looking?"

So whilst Pat is clearly not a physically attractive person, she is a very caring person. However, in paragraph five Pat's caring nature is shown to be tempered with a lack of social sensitivity: 'The old folks, Pat called them. Pat had done the notice in the library: Come and have fun giving a helping hand to the old folks. Adopt a granny. And the jokey cartoon drawing of a dear old bod with specs on the end of her nose and a shawl. One or two of the old people had been a bit sharp about that (line 20-23)'.

Mrs Rutter

Mrs Rutter's age is not directly stated but by deduction we can assume that she is in her mid-eighties. The story was written in 1984, if we assume that 1984 is the present day and she was 39 at the start of the war (line 329) when her husband was shot dead (line 165), Mrs Rutter would be approximately 84.

As mentioned above, Mrs Rutter is initially portrayed as a dear old lady, fragile and in need of help. Her house is filled with sentimental china ornaments: 'big-eyed flop-eared rabbits and beribboned kittens and flowery milkmaids and a pair of naked chubby children wearing daisy chains' (line 102). All these visual clues suggest a sweet and gentle-natured lady. However, as the story progresses layers are pealed back to reveal a more sinister nature. When Kerry discloses his plans to start at the garage after finishing school, Mrs Rutter responds with: "Well, I expect that's good steady money if you'd nothing special in mind. Sugar?" Here she demonstrates a demeaning and dismissive side. Later, talking of Pat, she passes further judgement: "She was down here last week. Ever such a nice person. Kind. It's sad she never married."

When she finally recounts the story of the crashed German plane, she displays a long-standing bitterness, an uncompromising sense of blamelessness and an utter lack of regret. She even recalls that she, along with others, took 'souvenirs' from the site of the crash, as if the incident was little more than a day trip. While the airman is left dying in the plane Mrs Rutter recounts how she attended to her chores before going back into the woods to 'have another look'.

We learn that the airman is not an old man as Mrs Rutter initially imagined but a young man, around the age of twenty and yet Mrs Rutter, oblivious to the irony of her words, states twice in the story that she has an empathy with young people. Once at line 170 before she has recounted the story of the German plane: "I like young people, I never had any children, it's been a loss that, I've got sympathy with young people." And at line 342, after having shared the German soldier's plight: "I like having someone young about the place, once in a while. I've got sympathy with young people."

That Mrs Rutter fails to recognise the irony of her words suggests that the young airman was, in her eyes, an almost sub-human adversary, not a living breathing person. When the children decide to leave she is almost stunned, unaware of their shock and revulsion: "Eh?' said the old woman. 'You're off are you?'... (line 340)'.

Language

The narrative passages within the body of the story switch style. Sometimes we are party to the author's words and at other times the narrative is written from Sandra's perspective. The author achieves this by alternating between two distinct methods. The first, which supplies the author's perspective, uses formal language, complex metaphors and pronouns in place of the characters' names. This creates a sense of detachment and adult authority. The second method, which supplies Sandra's perspective, uses truncated sentences and a simpler more casual use of words, suggestive of her age. The extracts below provide a good example:

The author as narrator:

Line 95: 'She seemed composed of circles, a cottage-loaf of a woman, with a face below which chins collapsed one into another, a creamy smiling pool of a face in which her eyes snapped and darted'.

Line 138: 'When she returned, the old woman was back in the armchair, a composite chintzy mass from which cushions oozed and her voice flowed softly on'.

Sandra as narrator:

Line 40: 'It was alright out here in the sunshine. Fine'.

Line 186: 'A place in the country. One day she would have a place in the country, but not like this. Sometime'.

The author uses metaphor liberally throughout the story, this serves to paint a very detailed visual picture. In line 96 the author describes Mrs Rutter's face as: '...a creamy smiling pool of a face...' and in line 116 describing the surroundings she writes: 'Beyond, the spinney reached up to the fence a no-man's-land of willowherb and thistle'. Simile is used to the same effect – line 128: 'a speck like a pin-head'; line 109: 'Her eyes investigate, quick as mice'.

Colloquial language is used throughout the story, both Sandra and Kerry speak in regional dialect (line 82): "Kerry Stevens you stupid-so-and-so, what d'you want to go and do that for, you <u>give me</u> the fright of my life." He grinned. "<u>I seen</u> you coming. Thought I might as well wait." Similarly, Mrs Rutter alternately addresses Sandra as 'my duck' or 'dear'.

The author uses repetition to emphasize the atmosphere. Towards the beginning of the story several permutations of 'sun' are repeated: Sunshine; sunburn; hair was hot from the sun; glinted in the sun. These are all words or phrases associated with lightness, they are not suggestive of the darkness which will manifest itself later in the story. By way of contrast in the penultimate paragraph the author repeats the word 'darkness'. This repetition serves to emphasize the horrors of what the two children have learnt: 'You could get people wrong and there was a darkness that was not the darkness of tree shadows and murky undergrowth... One moment you were walking in long grass with the sun on your hair and birds singing and the next you glimpsed darkness, an inescapable darkness. The darkness was out there and it was part of you....'

Darkness and light are used as metaphors for good and bad. At first the darkness is attached to Packer's End but later in the story we understand that the darkness refers to an 'inescapable darkness', that is, the darkness of human nature.

Themes

The Deception of Appearances

Perhaps the main theme running core to the story is that appearances are deceptive, things are not always as they may initially seem. The author first presents the scene as pretty, flower filled and sun-drenched, an innocuous atmosphere: .pollen summer grass that glinted in the sun'. However, she then introduces Packer's End, a complete contrast. The woods are menacing and full of folklore and horrors, both imagined and real: 'It was a rank place, all whippy saplings and brambles and a gully with a dumped mattress and bedstead... And, somewhere, presumably, the crumbling rusty scraps of metal and cloth and... bones?'.

The characters also follow this theme. At first we are lead to believe that Mrs Rutter is a 'dear old thing', however, later in the story she reveals her true colours when having found the dying airman she recounts her actions: "He was hurt pretty bad. He was kind of talking to himself... Dot said he's not going to last long, and a good job too, three of them that'll be. She'd been a VAD so she knew a bit about casualties, see'. Mrs Rutter licked her lips; she looked across at them, her eyes darting. 'Then we went back to the cottage". Far from being a 'dear old thing', Mrs Rutter shows herself to be unapologetically ruthless.

Similarly Kerry is initially presented as someone Sandra and her friends have no time for, Sandra certainly makes clear her disappointment when she realises that Kerry will be helping out with her at Mrs Rutter's: 'She wished there was Suzie to have a giggle with, not just Kerry Stevens'. He is described unsympathetically as having 'black licked-down hair' and 'slitty eyes', his chin is 'explosive with acne'. However, when he learns of the airman's plight his demeanour changes. He becomes physically and verbally demonstrative. His language becomes peppered with swear words. Appalled at the airman's treatment he says: "I'm not going near that old bitch again."

Sandra finally recognises Kerry as the young man he is, no longer is he someone to be 'not reckoned much on' and no longer does she perceive him as immature (line 216: 'She considered him, across the fence, over a chasm. Mum said boys matured later, in many ways'). In the penultimate paragraph the author divulges Sandra's new attitude:

She couldn't think of anything to say. He had grown; he had got older and larger. His anger eclipsed his acne, the patches of grease on his jeans, his lardy midriff. You could get people all wrong, she realised with alarm.

The final paragraph summarises this core theme: 'She walked behind him, through a world grown unreliable, in which flowers sparkle and birds sing but everything is not as it seems'.

The Darkness and the Light

This is an important theme, so much so that it is part of the story's title. There is a physical contrast between darkness and light: the journey in the sunshine and the darkness of Packer's End. But there is also the metaphorical contrast between darkness and light, the contrast between good and evil.

Looking Forward/Looking Back

In the story Sandra dreams of the future. Her imagined future is a simple one: to fall in love, to have a couple of children, to work as a secretary and to have a little cottage in the country. As she prepares for her visit to Mrs Rutter she muses innocently: 'Now, she would go to this old Mrs Rutter's and have a bit of a giggle with Susie and come home for tea and wash her hair. She would walk like this through the silken grass with the wind seething the corn and the secret invisible life of birds beside her in the hedge....' Here she paints an idyllic and undemanding picture of the immediate future, her thoughts are full of hopes and desires. This is in direct contrast to Mrs Rutter's retrospective thinking. Mrs Rutter speaks only of the past and she delivers her thoughts with bitterness and regret. Perhaps her thoughts remain in the past because after her husband's death, her life appears to have gone into stasis. She does not re-marry, she has no children and she continues residing in the marital home.

A Note on Stereotyping and Prejudice

Sandra reveals herself to hold a number of subliminal prejudices. Namely: People who help other people are not very nice looking, while people with platinum highlights and spike-heel suede boots are unlikely to offer community support. Similarly, when she reflects on events at Packer's End she recounts that the attackers of a young girl were 'two enormous blokes, sort of gypsy types'. Sandra slots herself into a very narrow stereotype with her dreams of secretarial work, becoming a home-maker and a mother. Her aversion to dirt and her concept of male work suggest an acceptance of really quite old-fashioned and gender divisive thinking.

Meanwhile Pat bundles all old people into a 'dear old thing' category, referring to them as 'the old folks' and encouraging support for the Good Neighbour's Club with the advert 'Adopt a granny'. Effectively, she defines people purely by their age.

Mrs Rutter's prejudice is transparent. She refers to the injured airman as 'that Jerry'; her self-professed empathy for young people evidently does not extend to the German.

29430808R00072

Printed in Great Britain
by Amazon

The Gender-Neutral

BABY NAME BOOK

OVER 1,000 UNISEX, ANDROGYNOUS, NON-GENDER NAMES